# THE SOCIETY OF ILLUSTRATORS
## TWENTY SIXTH ANNUAL OF
## AMERICAN ILLUSTRATION
# ILLUSTRATORS

EXHIBITION HELD IN THE GALLERIES OF
THE SOCIETY OF ILLUSTRATORS MUSEUM
OF AMERICAN ILLUSTRATION, 128 EAST
63RD STREET, NEW YORK, NEW YORK
FEBRUARY 1-APRIL 13, 1984.

**Society of Illustrators, Inc.**
**128 East 63rd Street, New York, N.Y. 10021**

ISBN 0-942604-05-9
Library of Congress Catalog Card Number 59-10849

Distributors to the trade in the United States:
Robert Silver Associates, 307 East 37th Street, New York, NY 10016

Distributors to the trade in Canada:
General Publishing Co. Ltd., 30 Lesmill Road, Don Mills, Ontario, Canada M3B 2T6

Distributed in Contintental Europe by:
Feffer and Simons, B.V., 170 Rijnkade, Weesp, Netherlands

Distributed throughout the rest of the world by:
Fleetbooks, S.A., c/o Feffer and Simons, Inc., 100 Park Avenue, New York, N.Y. 10017

Publisher: Madison Square Press, Inc., 10 East 23rd Street, New York, NY 10010

Art Weithas, Editor    Robert Anthony, Designer
Bernadette Evangelist and Charles Kreloff, Assistant Designers    Carnig Ermoyan, Mechanicals

Typography: Concept Typographic Services, Inc.    Printed in Japan.

# THE SOCIETY OF ILLUSTRATORS
# TWENTY SIXTH ANNUAL OF
# AMERICAN ILLUSTRATION
# ILLUSTRATORS

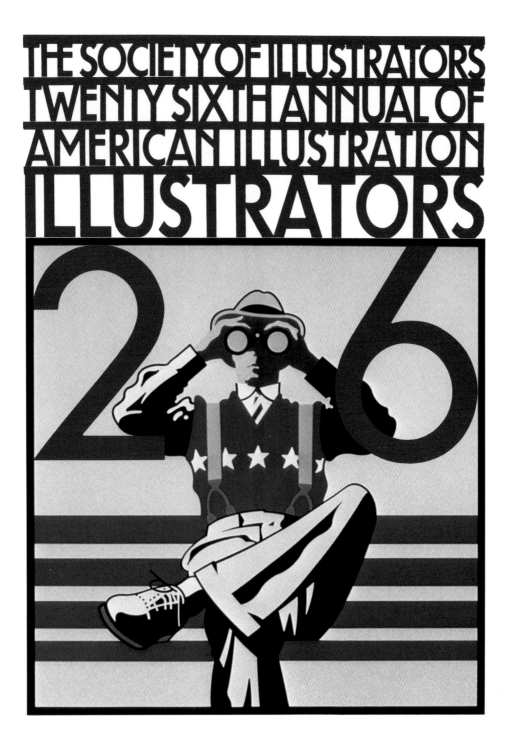

**1/26**

PUBLISHED FOR THE SOCIETY OF ILLUSTRATORS BY MADISON SQUARE PRESS, INC., NEW YORK 10010
DISTRIBUTED BY ROBERT SILVER ASSOCIATES, NEW YORK 10016

## Officers 1983-1984

| | |
|---|---|
| Honorary President | Stevan Dohanos |
| President | D. L. Cramer |
| Executive Vice-President | Walter Hortens |
| Vice President | Art Weithas |
| Treasurer | Nat Glattauer |
| Associate Treasurer | Georgia Froom |
| Secretary | Betty Fraser |
| House Chairman | Gerald McConnell |
| Past President | John Witt |

## Illustrators 26 Book Committee

| | |
|---|---|
| Produced for the Society by | Madison Square Press |
| Production and Advertising | Janet Weithas |
| Annual Editor | Art Weithas |
| Annual Designer | Robert Anthony |

## Illustrators 26 Show Committee

| | |
|---|---|
| Poster Artist | Marvin Mattelson |
| Poster Designer | Wendell Minor |
| Hanging Chairman | Wendell Minor |
| Executive Director | Terrence Brown |
| Exhibition Chairman | Roland Descombes |
| Exhibition Co-Chairman | Barnett Plotkin |
| House Manager | Norma Pimsler |
| Show Staff | Jill Bossert |
| | Carnig Ermoyan |
| | Anna Lee Fuchs |
| | Phyllis Harvey |
| | Jennifer Paul |
| | Fred Taraba |
| | Kathy Sachar |

## PRESIDENT'S MESSAGE

The Society of Illustrators is proud to begin its second quarter century of annual publications by presenting ILLUSTRATORS 26.

This book reproduces all of the works which were shown at the Society's Annual Show at the Society of Illustrators Museum of American Illustration in New York City. Out of 6,200 entires, 36 distinguished jurors have selected the numerous exciting works which appear herein.

Anyone optimistic about the future of illustration will find reinforcement in these pages. Once again we can see the illustrator filling a role as the interpreter of culture, sometimes with a vengeance. All works done in color have been faithfully reproduced in color.

My thanks to the jurors, the people who hung the show, the many people who worked on this first-rate book, and most of all, to the many artists who shared their vision of our world with us.

D. L. CRAMER, Ph.D.
*President, Society of Illustrators*

Illustration: Paul Calle

# NEW ACQUISITIONS

## NEW ACQUISITIONS FOR THE PERMANENT COLLECTION OF THE SOCIETY OF ILLUSTRATORS MUSEUM OF AMERICAN ILLUSTRATION

**S**ixty-eight newly acquired paintings and drawings were exhibited in the Museum galleries from November 9 to December 2, 1983. Many of the pieces were of major importance including J.C. Leyendecker, Ben Stahl, Walter Biggs, Noel Sickles, Robert Riggs and Anton Otto Fischer.

These plus the more than a thousand works of art by over 425 illustrators comprise the most representative and comprehensive collection of American illustration by any museum devoted entirely to this art. Its preservation makes possible the enjoyment of illustration for present and future generations. The art was obtained through donations, purchase and permanent loan.

More and more of the collection is now on display, not only at the Society, but in traveling exhibitions and loans to other museums. Over 14% of the collection was displayed in 1983-84. Much of the collection was available to students and professionals for study and research.

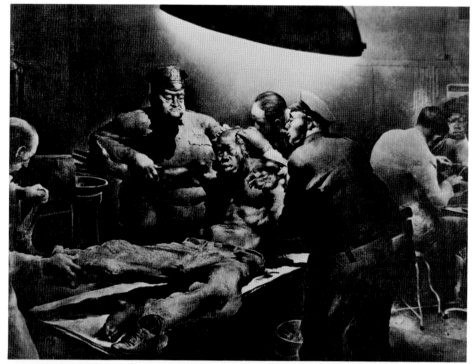

Robert Riggs (1896-1970), "Accident Ward," donated by Mr. & Mrs. Albert Gold.

J. C. Leyendecker, "Good Clothes," donated by Lowell M. Schulman.

Walter Biggs, "The Preacher," donated by Janet & Art Weithas.

**Ben Stahl** (b. 1910), "She Turned A Wilderness into a Home," donated by Daniel W. Keefe.

**Daniel Schwartz** (b. 1929), "Suffragette Marchers,"
*McCall's Magazine*, 1961, donated anonymously.

# NEW ACQUISITIONS

The collection of contemporary illustration, potentially our most important resource, grew through contributions by John Berkey, Bob Crofut, Richard Ely, George Guzzi, Philip Miller, Cal Sacks and Dan Schwartz.

Terry Brown, our former curator, has become the new Director of the Society of Illustrators, succeeding Arpi Ermoyan, who retired after devoting eighteen years of selfless service to the Society.

She leaves many, many friends who will always wish her well and who are deeply appreciative of her contributions to the Society and her concern for the members.

During Terry Brown's tenure as curator, he catalogued, collated, had photographed and recorded the entire Museum collection in addition to his other myriad duties.

John Moodie continues as Chairman of the Permanent Collection. It is largely through his efforts that the present collection has attained the growth and stature that it now enjoys.

The Museum Committee consists of Robert H. Blattner, Mitchell Hooks, Wendell Minor, John Moodie, Howard Munce, Walt Reed, Murray Tinkelman, John Witt and Art Weithas, Chairman.

The following made generous contributions: Robert H. Blattner, Bob Crozier and family, Mr. and Mrs. Ben Eisenstadt, Mac S. Fisher, Mr. and Mrs. Al Gold, Carla Kenny, George Noah Payne, Frances C. Rooff and Beverly and Ray Sachs.

Thanks to the following for their additions of illustrations on Permanent Loan: The Tenafly New Jersey Public Library (Harvey Dunn), Stephan Fay and Stephanie Fay Arpajian (Clark Fay).

Funds contributed by the members of the Society and by supporting corporations and friends have made possible the purchase of works by Anton Otto Fischer, Arthur B. Frost, Frederick G. Cooper and Henry Raleigh.

The Society is pleased to recognize as patrons the following for their generous contributions to the collection: Lowell M. Schulman, Everett Raymond Kinstler, Charles E. Rowe, Mr. and Mrs. Albert Gold, Frederic R. Gruger, Jr., Mrs. Howard Scott and Yale University Art Gallery.

The Society continues its association with the families of past illustrators. Through them, many fine and biographically important items have been added to the archives. We are indebted to Mrs. Stephen Rountree Otis (Sam Otis), Dorothy W. Rose (Carl Rose), Mrs. Howard Scott and Judith Hempe Smulcheski (Watson Barratt).

Anton Otto Fischer (1882-1962), "Tugboat Annie," *The Saturday Evening Post*, The J. Walter Thompson Company Purchase Fund.

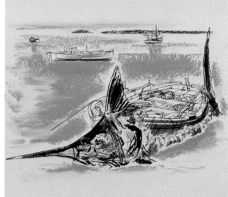

Noel Sickles (1911-1982), "The Marlin Breaks Water," The Old Man and The Sea by Ernest Hemingway, *Life Magazine*, 1952, donated by Mrs. Noel Sickles.

Constantin Alajalov (b. 1900), "The Ground Breaking," *The New Yorker*, J. Walter Thompson Company Purchase Fund.

# HALL OF FAME AWARD

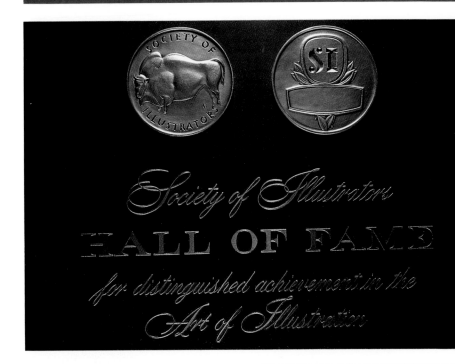

Each year the Society of Illustrators presents its Hall of Fame award to three distinguished illustrators. This year's awards were received by:

Nesya Moran McMein (1890-1944) was a legend in her own time. She was both a great artist and a famous social figure of the '20s and '30s. Famous for her covers of *McCall's* Magazine 1923-36, she also painted many of the great celebrities of the period such as Helen Hayes, Noel Coward.

James W. Williamson (1899-1983) was known to everyone as "Jimmy." He had a delightful sense of humor. He was probably best known for his advertising campaigns for Arrow Shirts, Ford Motors, and for his illustrations in *The Saturday Evening Post* for Philip Wylie's stories.

John LaGatta (1894-1977) is best known as a painter of elegant people, particularly women. He showed a full appreciation of the female figure in his illustrations. His work was in great demand by all the magazines of his day.

## Hall of Fame Chairman
Willis Pyle

## Hall of Fame Committee
Past Presidents of the Society

| | |
|---|---|
| Walter Brooks | Alvin J. Pimsler |
| Harry Carter | Warren Rogers |
| Stevan Dohanos | William Schneider |
| Tran Mawicke | Shannon Stirnweis |
| Charles McVicker | David K. Stone |
| John A. Moodie | John Witt |
| Howard Munce | |

## Previous Hall of Fame Award Winners
Norman Rockwell 1958
Dean Cornwell 1959
Harold von Schmidt 1959
Fred Cooper 1960
Floyd Davis 1961
Edward Wilson 1962
Walter Biggs 1963
Arthur William Brown 1964
Al Parker 1965
Al Dorne 1966
Robert Fawcett 1967
Peter Helck 1968
Austin Briggs 1969
Rube Goldberg 1970
Stevan Dohanos 1971
Ray Prohaska 1972
Jon Whitcomb 1973
Tom Lovell 1974
Charles Dana Gibson* 1974
N.C. Wyeth* 1974
Bernie Fuchs 1975
Maxfield Parrish* 1975
Howard Pyle* 1975
John Falter 1976
Winslow Homer* 1976
Harvey Dunn* 1976
Robert Peak 1977
Wallace Morgan* 1977
J.C. Leyendecker* 1977
Coby Whitmore 1978
Norman Price* 1978
Frederic Remington* 1978
Ben Stahl 1979
Edwin Austin Abbey* 1979
Lorraine Fox* 1979
Saul Tepper 1980
Howard Chandler Christy* 1980
James Montgomery Flagg* 1980
Stan Galli 1981
Frederic R. Gruger* 1981
John Gannam* 1981
John Clymer 1982
Henry P. Raleigh* 1982
Eric (Carl Erickson)* 1982
Mark English 1983
Noel Sickles* 1983
Franklin Booth* 1983

*presented posthumously

## NEYSA MORAN McMEIN (1890-1949)

Neysa McMein was a legend in her own time—as a great artist and as one of the most fabulous social figures in the '20s and '30s. At a birthday party for Irene Castle she met her future husband, John Baragwanath. To him she was "striking, fairly tall, with a fine figure, high cheekbones, greenish eyes, dark lashes and brows and a tumbling mass of untidy blond hair."

The next time they met was at her studio in the Hotel des Artistes. Jascha Heifitz was at one of her double pianos while Heywood Broun and George F. Kaufman played poker. Aspiring actresses lounged on the sofa, Vanderbilts and Pulitzers drifted about and Neysa worked though it all, surrounded by clouds of pastel dust. Her great friend Noel Coward said she had a "unique talent for living." She also had a great talent for drawing—especially pretty girls.

Born Marjorie Moran McMein in Quincy, Illinois, she had hoped to have a musical career. Family finances altered her plans, but she was able to support herself with her music while studying at the Chicago Art Institute. Weary of her first job sketching hats for the Gage Brothers Department Store, Marjorie joined a vaudeville troupe to write songs and music. The act folded, but she had gotten to New York City. There she sold her first picture of a pretty girl for $75.

Miss McMein felt she needed a new name for her new life—a numerologist told her Marjorie was an unlucky one. She chose the name of an Arabian horse she'd once seen and admired: Neysa. Whether it was numerology or talent, from then on Neysa was a success. She painted her first cover for *The Saturday Evening Post* in 1915, the same year she joined the Society of Illustrators. Covers for *Woman's Home Companion, Collier's* and *McClure's* followed, as well as advertising assignments for clients such as Cadillac and Palmolive.

The McMein girls were a departure from the cutesy, baby-doll look that was fashionable at the time. Her women were beautiful, of course. And they had intelligence and grace —a cool, commanding sense of themselves. It was not simply youth on their side like the dimpled, bee-stung frothy girls that preceded them. Her 1918 Red Cross girl is not only luminous in her dark beauty, she is also caring, concerned. A *Post* cover of 1921 depicts a gorgeous woman with an armful of flowers. There's not a simper in sight; in fact, her look is almost challenging. And Neysa's stunning Lucky Strike bride exudes confidence as she exhales, "*I do.*"

In 1923 she painted her first *McCall's* cover. From 1924 to 1936 she held an exclusive contract with the magazine to do their covers, a procession of lovely women, month after month, all executed in the whirl of Neysa's extraordinary social life. In 1924, she also found time to have a daughter, Joan. Robert Benchley, Dorothy Parker, Charlie Chaplin and Bernard Baruch milled around as Bea Lillie sang "There are Fairies at the Bottom of My Garden," and Neysa worked. In addition to the cool beauties for *McCall's*, she specialized in nudes, often using three models for one piece: one for the head, one for the torso and one for the legs!

Though she fancied elephant riding at Ringling Brothers Circus opening nights and enjoyed heavyweight bouts with Charlie McArthur, Neysa McMein was also concerned with the welfare of others. During the World Wars she produced posters both in the United States and in France. And for years her illustrations for The New York Times Hundred Neediest Cases helped to raise large sums of money for the poor each Christmas. The Greater New York Fund and the Council Against Intolerance in America were also beneficiaries of her care for the less fortunate.

Her interest in new, artistic talent often moved her to acts of generosity. For example, because she was impressed with the nascent talent of a young dishwasher, Neysa supported him in his studies. He went on to win the Prix de Rome.

When her contract with *McCall's* expired—color photography had supplanted her glorious, but expensive pastels—she turned to oil portraiture. Jack Dempsey, President Warren G. Harding, Chief Justice Charles Evans Hughes and Charlie Chaplin sat for her, as well as the country's most prominent women, including Edna St. Vincent Millay and Katherine Cornell.

She died in 1949 after a brief illness. About her Noel Coward wrote: "Neysa was one of the rare people in the world whose genius for friendship could pierce through all facades, surmount all defenses, and find its way immediately and unerringly to the secret heart."

As an appreciation of her life and work, the Whitney Museum of American Art has established a memorial fund in her honor which is used to purchase work by living American artists.

Whether she was dancing with Clifton Webb or laughing with Edgar Bergen, playwriting with her husband or meeting Rajahs with Peggy Pulitzer, creating visions of pastel beauty or immortalizing Presidents in oil, she was an original.

*Jill Bossert*

Neysa McMein, "Seated Nude," Courtesy, the Society of Illustrators Museum of American Illustration, donated by the artist.

## JAMES WILLIAMSON (1899-1983)

Jimmy Williamson was never known as Mr. Williamson. A few close friends, on occasion, called him Jim. Otherwise he was known as Jimmy Williamson, the artist illustrator par excellence.

A guy of medium stature with a rather sharp quizzical face, he wore metal-framed glasses which gave the impression that he had been born with them on and that they had just grown along with him. His sense of humor was a delight, a mixture of kindness and humor that offended no one, but made everyone smile. Also, most of his jokes were about himself. One of the few cracks I ever heard him make about someone else was a quip he dropped about Gene Davis. Gene had been top art director at Young & Rubicam where he handled several big accounts which Jimmy Williamson worked on (Packard and Arrow Shirts). Gene was a fastidious dresser with exquisite taste. His clothes were all made for him by the top designers. He frequented the best restaurants (with Jimmy Williamson), and always wore a dark red carnation in his buttonhole. Sometime later, when Gene was art director of *Good Housekeeping* magazine, the bombshell news was dropped on us that Gene had enlisted as a captain in the U.S. Marines. Said Jimmy, "He won't be a leatherneck, he'll be a suedeneck."

I first met Jimmy Williamson when I was assistant art director to Gene Davis. I was 24 years old at the time and fresh out of art school. Jimmy Williamson was 35. I thought he was an old man. It was at this time that I learned that he thought he was color blind. I don't think that he wanted to flaunt this flaw to Gene. One day the door opened to Gene's office, which I shared with him, and in popped Jimmy Williamson's head, forehead furrowed and eyebrows raised. "Where is he?" Jimmy asked. I told him Gene was in a meeting and would be gone for some time. "Good," he said, "I wonder if you'd help me?" The mere thought that I could help the great Jimmy Williamson made my head balloon like a watermelon sittin' in the sun. He said, "I'm color blind and I wonder if you'd check out the color of these shirts for me?" He had an illustration for an Arrow Shirt ad and an armfull of shirts. The illustration was some kind of an outing with a lot of guys wearing Arrow Shirts. The shirts weren't bad. I got

out some opaque colors, mixed them up and he filled them in. I never felt like such a big shot in my life. He thanked me profusely and retired. He wasn't really color blind.

James W. Williamson was born on Cumings Street, in the Bemis Park section of Omaha, in September, 1899, an unlikely place for such a talent to emerge. From the beginning he was fascinated with penmanship and drawing and by the time he was four he was scratching on everything with anything that would make a mark.

His mother believed his bent for drawing was the result of an electric shock received in the bathroom and that it would lead to nothing but penury and starvation. Nevertheless, he continued his scratching, and became intrigued with Howard Pyle's pen technique, which he copied. His first fame came with an honorable mention in the St. Nicholas League.

At age eleven he was told by a grade school teacher that he was color blind, the unfounded notion he carried with him the rest of his life.

During his teens he continued to draw and was influenced by contemporary stars Herbert Davis, Franklin Booth and Carl Erickson.

In September of 1918 Jimmy went to a training camp in Ithaca, N.Y. However, the war ended in December and he was out of a job again.

Poking around New York for a year, he did a few cartoons for *Life* and *Judge*. Then, in September of 1919, he went to Yale and got on the college humor sheet, *The Record*.

There he worked on staff with Reggie Marsh and Bill Benton.

Around 1923, by chance, he broke into commercial art doing a series of ads for Kelly Springfield Tires that appeared in *Vanity Fair*. These ads were so successful that Vaughn Flannery at N.W. Ayer put him under contract to Ford Motor Company. Also, about this time, story illustration opened up with Williamson doing work for Henry Quinan at *Woman's Home Companion* and for Joe Platt at *The Delineator*.

Then, in 1931, Vaughn Flannery, having moved from N.W. Ayer to Young & Rubicam, pegged Williamson for more commercial work. He was off and running in the ad game. He worked with Chan Lane, Butch Smith, Ernie Button, Gene Davis, Ted Patrick, Jack Anthony, Hugh White, Bill Reimers and yours truly at Y & R. He also worked with Charlie Coiner and Gordon Wilber at Ayer, and Dan Keefe and Jack Tinker at McCann Erickson.

In 1933, he tried a stint of teaching at the Arts Students League, but gave it up as a bad job.

1942 found him involved in the war effort on a top secret mission so hush-hush that little is known about it, except that he trained in Canada, was smuggled out to spend a year in Istanbul, six months in Cairo and fifteen months in Rome.

In 1946 he returned to New York and the advertising business where he got a warm welcome from all his old friends.

New careers kept bubbling up. Nelson Gruppo sent him a series of stories to illustrate. Ken Stuart and Bob Blattner of *Reader's Digest* gave him a steady stream of most amusing work. Then came a letter from Stevan Dohanos saying that a jury of his peers had designated him for the Sanford Low Collection of Illustration at the New Britain Museum of American Art, a feather he proudly wore in his cap to the very end.

In 1952 Jimmy Williamson moved to Santurce in Puerto Rico, a suburb of San Juan. He no longer was willing to put up with the cold winters of New England. In Puerto Rico's incredible climate he continued to work and enjoy life until his recent death. To the very end, he was charming, witty, debonair and always a gentleman.

*Bill Kammer*

James W. Williamson, "She Wanted a Hero," by Philip Wylie, *The Saturday Evening Post*.

## JOHN LA GATTA (1894-1977)

John LaGatta is best known for his paintings of beautiful people. His female figures in particular were elegant and provocative at the same time. But the glamorous world he created in his editorial art was not initially his source of income. After studying art at the Chase School, N.Y. School of Fine and Applied Arts, Parsons and the Art Students League, he first earned his living doing advertising illustration.

Though very successful in this field, drawing products and product-oriented situations bored him, so he closed his New York studio for a year and moved to Woodstock, New York, in order to develop a portfolio of magazine illustrations that concentrated on beautiful women.

His lovely wife, Florence, an artist herself, became his model during that year, as well as his advisor. She remained his advisor throughout their 58 years of marriage, a fairly difficult assignment I would imagine, for LaGatta was known to have strong opinions which he was not afraid to voice.

The Woodstock experiment was so successful that in a very short time his work was used regularly by such publications as Cosmopolitan, Ladies' Home Journal and Redbook.

LaGatta masterfully depicted the country club set in art form, as John O'Hara did in word form.

John LaGatta was born in Naples, Italy, on May 26, 1894. After his mother's death his father moved John and his sister to Brazil, South America, and thereafter to New York City. LaGatta's father was a businessman and a designer of jewelry. He was against John's becoming an artist, but when offers of scholarships to art schools came in he relented.

John and his wife originally lived on Bank Street in Greenwich Village, New York, later at 1 West 67 Street (the Hotel des Artistes). They had a home and studio at Sands Point, Long Island, and a dramatic summer estate, designed by LaGatta, on Mt. Overlook, near Woodstock, New York.

The demand for romantic illustration decreased for awhile with the advent of World War II. The LaGattas moved to Santa Monica, California, in 1941. There John

started to paint for himself—portraits, landscapes, etc.—and loved it. He began teaching when he was 68 years old, sharing his vast knowledge of illustration with the students at Art Center in Los Angeles. He painted and taught on and off until his death at the age of 83.

John LaGatta was unique, his style completely his own. His artwork was admired by the public and applauded by his fellow illustrators. The Society of Illustrators is honored to include his name with the other greats in its Hall of Fame.

*John A. Moodie*
Chairman, SI Permanent
Collection Committee

John LaGatta, "Dr. McVane, M.D.," by Philip Wylie, *Redbook Magazine*, 1938, donated by Mr. & Mrs. Herman Schoppe.

## HAMILTON KING AWARD

The Hamilton King Award is given each year for the finest illustration by a member of the Society of Illustrators. The 1984 award winner is Braldt Bralds.

### 1984 Hamilton King Award Jurors

Robert Cuevas
Roland Descombs
Mitchell Hooks
Howard Koslow
Charles McVicker
Barnett Plotkin
Warren Rogers
Eileen Hedy Schultz
Shannon Stirnweis

### Hamilton King Award Winners

## HAMILTON KING AWARD 1984

### BRALDT BRALDS (b. 1951)
*Interviewed by Terry Brown*

**Terry Brown** Braldt, you're a relative new-comer to the field of American Illustration but have already reached "star" status, congratulations!

**Braldt Bralds** I still find it hard to acknowledge a statement like that, but thank you.

**TB** Your Hamilton King Award winning work typifies your mixture of craft and thought. How did it come about?

**BB** I was given the assignment to illustrate "Cuba Libre" (a rum & coke drink) for the Hotel Barmen's Association of Japan's calendar by their art director, Shinichiro Tora. My approach was, I find, a literal but symbolic interpretation of the two words. Cuba, symbolized by a smoking Havana cigar in an ashtray...the smoke just to give a feeling of presence without showing a figure...Libre, a free white dove flying towards the sunlight.

**TB** Was the setting also an interpretation?

**BB** Yes, a simple island café type situation, a place to have a drink. The "Cuba" part is shown in shadow, the "Libre" part in bright sunlight.

**TB** And Mr. Tora was pleased with the outcome?

**BB** Actually, he was more pleased than I was. I felt the piece didn't quite come out the way I had seen it in my mind and I had an urge to start it all over again. Thank God I didn't!

**TB** Are you generally satisfied with your work?

**BB** Not really. I think that most artists like to paint differently from what they are doing. It's hard to be crazy about your own work after struggling with it for a long time. I never find it easy. I'm more tolerant with the work of others and admire what is different from what I do.

**TB** Your amazing success in such a short time certainly shows that many people appreciate your work. How long have you been working in the U.S.?

**BB** Since 1980. My wife, Charlotte, and I came to New York to stay here for two months as a tryout and to get some feedback on my portfolio. At the suggestion of one of my clients in Europe I went to visit Milton Newborn who, together with Dick Hess, encouraged me to move to New York. Milton said: "When you do, I'd be delighted to rep you."

**TB** Has Milton been important to your success?

**BB** Yes, he has been very important in my career. I would say almost to the degree that I could not have done it without him in such a short period of time. We have a very professional/personal relationship. He had a stronger belief in me than I ever had about myself and especially during this past year which has been one fun job after another.

**TB** To have reached your level of craft and talent, you must have had some artists to whom you looked up.

**BB** Yes, I did. As a matter of fact it would be quite a list to try to name them all. But to mention a few, I admired a great deal (and still do!) the work of Dick Hess, Wilson McLean, David Wilcox, Bob Giusti and Brad Holland. But my earliest experience with illustration was through the ads for the Famous Artists School with Rockwell, Al Dorne and others. My father didn't really believe in an art career. He felt the business was too shaky to make a living in it.

**TB** What about art school?

**BB** My only art education was mechanical drawing in school and on the job as a type-setter in a local printing shop where we designed local announcements, letterheads and gallery posters. Ever since, I have been crazy about typography.

**TB** This was in your hometown of Rotterdam (Holland)?

**BB** That is where I grew up. Later I started working for an advertising agency there as a junior designer and illustrator which I did for two years, after which I started my free-lance career.

**TB** Were you able to incorporate your own drawings into the designs?

**BB** I often did and basically that is how I got into the field of illustration.

**TB** Do they have a different approach to freelance illustration there?

**BB** Definitely, there is not as much respect for the profession as there is in England and America. I did mostly product oriented

Braldt Bralds, "Cuba Libre," Calendar art (June, 1983) for The Hotel Barmen's Association (Japan).

illustrations and when I would make enough money doing them I could afford to do an editorial job here and there and have some fun with it. After a while, I felt a strong desire to expand.

**TB** You've proved that you are very adept at painting oils on masonite. Is that your favorite media?

**BB** Yes, absolutely, I tried acrylics with some success but couldn't stand it. Oils feel right and come easily and I find that I can do most everything with them.

**TB** The incredible detail in your work is one of its strongest assets. Does that come easily?

**BB** The only thing that comes easily for me is to accept a job and to deliver a job. Everything in between is frustration and I think that is how my style evolved. In painting each small area, I have to be satisfied that it can stand on its own, before I move to another area. It's the fear of being ashamed

when the final painting doesn't look good that makes my work look the way it does.

**TB** As an instructor at SVA, do you see the same diligence and patience in your students?

**BB** Not generally. Too many are looking for the magic trick to success and instant gratification.

**TB** Will you continue to teach?

**BB** Yes, it has been a great learning experience for me. It taught me that even without art school training, I did know a hell of a lot more about the profession than I gave myself credit for.

**TB** Have you thought about branching out into gallery painting?

**BB** Not right now, I'm enjoying illustrating too much. But it feels good to know that fantasy is out there. Certainly there would be fewer boundaries in that market.

**TB** And your eloquent style, will we continue to see that in the future?

**BB** I think so. Although I try to change and grow it will probably look as it does now anyway. I do love it. Maybe at some point it will get boring, but I haven't reached that yet, and if I do there will be another goal to reach for.

**TB** Any speculation on that goal?

**BB** Well, sometimes I feel a desperate need to be gutsy enough to be a kid again and to get rid of my tiny brushes and splash around on a huge canvas...and be spontaneous just for the sake of making a mark...just for myself. When the day comes that I have enough space to do that, I certainly will!

Braldt's last comment reflects on his own perspective of his work. He is a man so good at what he does, yet he has unborn ideas of new goals to reach. His dedication to make perfect the style and concept he has chosen for today is the mark he has made on American Illustration.

# JURY

**CAROL DONNER,** CHAIRMAN

Freelance illustrator specializing in medical illustration.

**GRACE D. CLARKE**

Publisher, Runcible Press, a children's book packager. Guest instructor, Sarah Lawrence College.

**MICHAEL DORET**

Freelance lettering artist/designer/illustrator.

**GARY KELLEY**

Illustrator, Vice President, Hellman Associates. Medal winner in Society Annual Exhibitions, exhibited in U.S., Japan and South America.

**ELWOOD SMITH**

Freelance illustrator. Award winning illustrations for advertising and publishing.

**HODGES SOILEAU**

Freelance illustrator.

**JÖZEF SUMICHRAST**

Freelance illustrator. Medals from the Society and the NY Art Directors Club. Exhibited throughout North America and Europe.

**BOB ZIERING**

Freelance illustrator. One-man show at the Society of Illustrators.

**PAUL DAVIS**

Freelance illustrator.

1

ARTIST: **MATT MAHURIN**    ART DIRECTOR: STEVEN DOYLE    MAGAZINE: ROLLING STONE

**GOLD MEDAL**

**2**

ARTIST: **WILLIAM LOW**    ART DIRECTOR: THOMAS RUIS    MAGAZINE: NEW YORK DAILY NEWS

**SILVER MEDAL**

**3**

ARTIST: **BRAD HOLLAND**     ART DIRECTOR: SKIP WILLIAMSON     MAGAZINE: PLAYBOY

**SILVER MEDAL**

**4**

ARTIST: **GUY BILLOUT**    ART DIRECTOR: DEREK W. UNGLESS    MAGAZINE: ROLLING STONE

**SILVER MEDAL**

JOHN RUSH

**6**

ARTIST: **JOHN CRAIG**
ART DIRECTOR: BETT McLEAN/ANDREW EPSTEIN
MAGAZINE: THE BEST OF BUSINESS

**7**

ARTIST: **BURT SILVERMAN**    ART DIRECTOR: LEONARD WOLFE    MAGAZINE: DISCOVER

**8**

ARTIST: **GUY BILLOUT**
ART DIRECTOR: JUDY GARLAN
MAGAZINE: THE ATLANTIC MONTHLY

**9**

ARTIST: **KENT BARTON**
ART DIRECTOR: KENT BARTON
MAGAZINE: THE MIAMI
HERALD

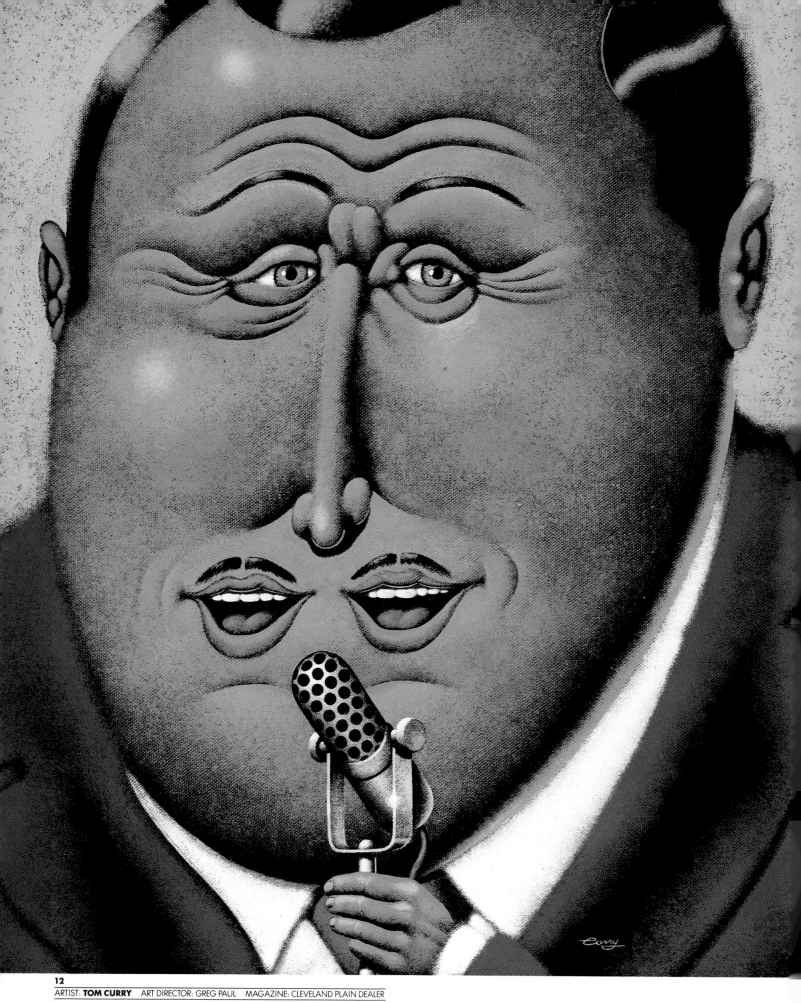

**12**
ARTIST: **TOM CURRY**    ART DIRECTOR: GREG PAUL    MAGAZINE: CLEVELAND PLAIN DEALER

ARTIST: **JOSÉ CRUZ**    ART DIRECTOR: JUDY GARLAN    MAGAZINE: THE ATLANTIC MONTHLY

**15**
ARTIST: **BARRON STOREY**   ART DIRECTOR: JAN ADKINS   MAGAZINE: NATIONAL GEOGRAPHIC

**16**
ARTIST: **WENDELL MINOR**   ART DIRECTOR: JUDY GARLAN   MAGAZINE: THE ATLANTIC MONTHLY

**17**

ARTIST: **MARK ENGLISH**

ART DIRECTOR: HERB BLEIWEISS
MAGAZINE: GOOD HOUSEKEEPING

**18**

ARTIST: **MARSHALL ARISMAN**

ART DIRECTOR: NANCY DUCKWORTH
MAGAZINE: CALIFORNIA

**19**
ARTIST: **GREGORY MANCHESS**
ART DIRECTOR: PATRICK DEFFENBAUGH
MAGAZINE: OMNI

**20**
ARTIST: **BURT SILVERMAN**
ART DIRECTOR: RUDOLPH HOGLUND
MAGAZINE: TIME

**21**
ARTIST: **KENT BARTON**
ART DIRECTOR: KENT BARTON
MAGAZINE: THE MIAMI HERALD

**22**
ARTIST: **THOMAS WOODRUFF**
ART DIRECTOR: RANDY L. DUNBAR
MAGAZINE: HEALTH

**23**
ARTIST: **MARVIN MATTELSON**
ART DIRECTOR: KENNETH SURABIAN
MAGAZINE: DATAMATION

ARTIST: **MARSHALL ARISMAN**    ART DIRECTOR: RONN CAMPISI    MAGAZINE: BOSTON GLOBE

**25**
ARTIST: **KENT BARTON**
ART DIRECTOR: KENT BARTON
MAGAZINE: THE MIAMI HERALD

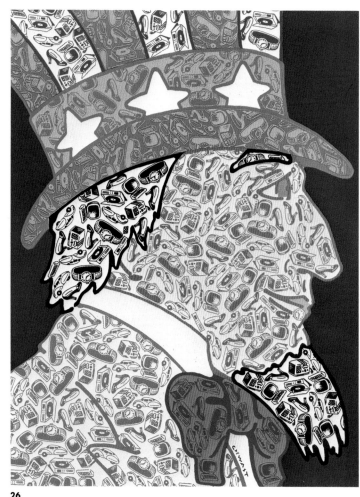

**26**
ARTIST: **SEYMOUR CHWAST**
ART DIRECTOR: JUDY GARLAN
MAGAZINE: THE ATLANTIC MONTHLY

**27**
ARTIST: **NOVLE ROGERS**    ART DIRECTOR: BROC SEARS    MAGAZINE: THE DALLAS MORNING NEWS

**28**
ARTIST: **BARRON STOREY**

ART DIRECTOR: JAN ADKINS
MAGAZINE: NATIONAL GEOGRAPHIC

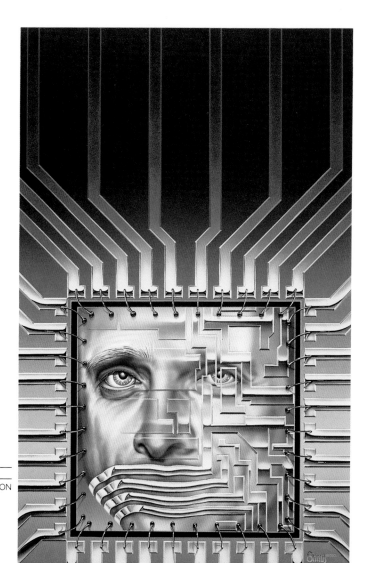

**29**
ARTIST: **BARCLAY SHAW**

ART DIRECTOR: ELIZABETH WOODSON
MAGAZINE: OMNI

**30**

ARTIST: **WM. A. MOTTA**

ART DIRECTOR: WM. A. MOTTA    MAGAZINE: ROAD & TRACK

**31**

ARTIST: **YOSHIHIRO INOMOTO**

ART DIRECTOR: WM. A. MOTTA
MAGAZINE: ROAD & TRACK

**32**
ARTIST: **MATT MAHURIN**
ART DIRECTOR: RUDOLPH HOGLUND/IRENE RAMP
MAGAZINE: TIME

**33**
ARTIST: **DAVE BHANG**
ART DIRECTOR: MASSIS ARARADIAN
MAGAZINE: LOS ANGELES HERALD EXAMINER

**34**
ARTIST: **GEORGE MENCH**
ART DIRECTOR: ALFRED ZELCER
MAGAZINE: PHILADELPHIA

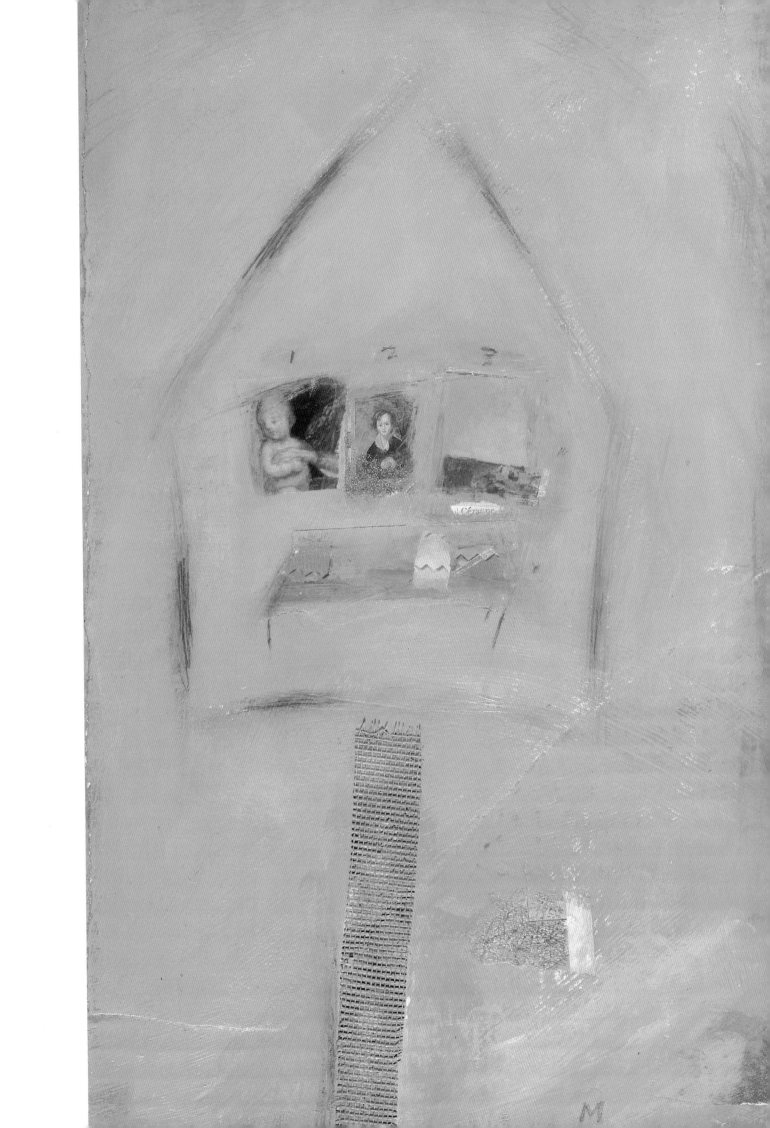

35
ARTIST: **CHRISTOPHER CALLE**
ART DIRECTOR: NORMAN HOTZ
MAGAZINE: READER'S DIGEST

36
ARTIST: **PATRICK McDONNELL**
ART DIRECTOR: DEIRDRE COSTA MAJOR
MAGAZINE: PARENTS

**37**
ARTIST: **KAREN FARYNIAK**
CLIENT: COLOR SERVICES

**38**
ARTIST: **C.F. PAYNE**
ART DIRECTOR: FRED WOODWARD
MAGAZINE: WESTWARD

ARTIST: **LARRY RIVERS** ART DIRECTOR: TOM STAEBLER/KERIG POPE MAGAZINE: PLAYBOY

**42**
ARTIST: **EDWARD SOREL**
ART DIRECTOR: LLOYD ZIFF
MAGAZINE: VANITY FAIR

**43**
ARTIST: **DAVID LEVINE**
ART DIRECTOR: LLOYD ZIFF
MAGAZINE: VANITY FAIR

**44**
ARTIST: **ALAN E. COBER**
ART DIRECTOR: JUDY GARLAN
MAGAZINE: THE ATLANTIC MONTHLY

**45**
ARTIST: **VIVIENNE FLESHER**
ART DIRECTOR: FRED WOODWARD
MAGAZINE: TEXAS MONTHLY

ARTIST: **BARBARA NESSIM**    ART DIRECTOR: RONN CAMPISI    MAGAZINE: BOSTON GLOBE

**47**

ARTIST: **DAVID NOYES**

ART DIRECTOR: ANTHONY LYLE
MAGAZINE: THE PENNSYLVANIA GAZETTE

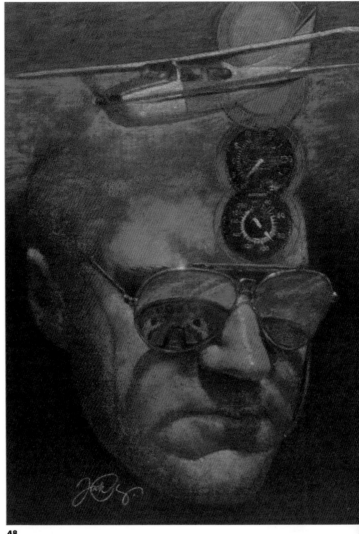

**48**

ARTIST: **JACK PARDUE**

ART DIRECTOR: ART DAVIS/NANCY MENDEZ
MAGAZINE: AOPA PILOT

**49**

ARTIST: **GUY GLADWELL**

ART DIRECTOR: JUDY GARLAN
MAGAZINE: THE ATLANTIC MONTHLY

**50**

ARTIST: **GUY GLADWELL**

ART DIRECTOR: JUDY GARLAN
MAGAZINE: THE ATLANTIC MONTHLY

ARTIST: **DALE GOTTLIEB**   ART DIRECTOR: TINA ADAMEK   MAGAZINE: POSTGRADUATE MEDICINE

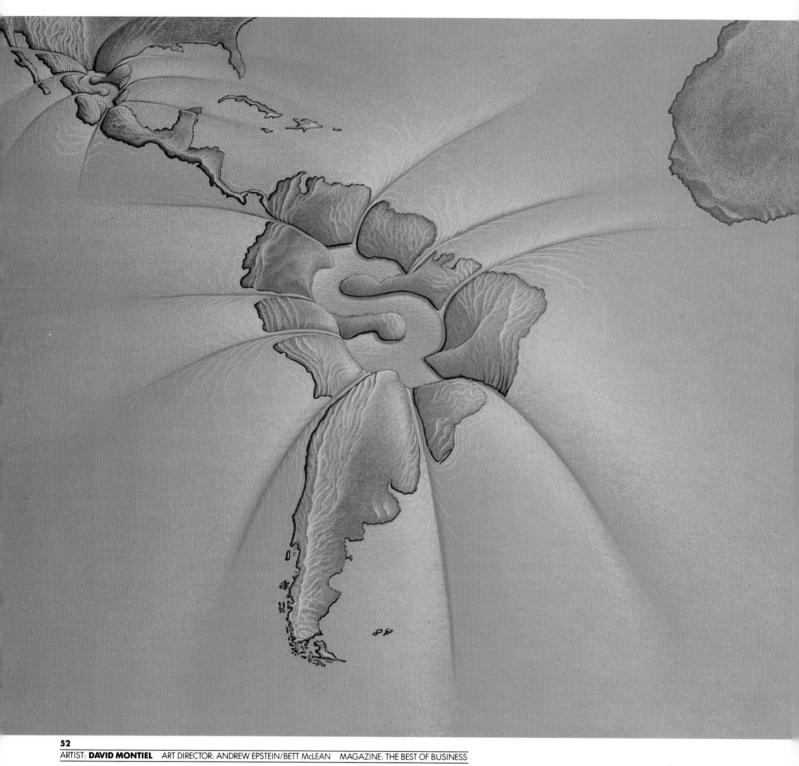

**52**
ARTIST: **DAVID MONTIEL**   ART DIRECTOR: ANDREW EPSTEIN/BETT McLEAN   MAGAZINE: THE BEST OF BUSINESS

**53**
ARTIST: **JAMES NOEL SMITH**    ART DIRECTOR: FRED WOODWARD    MAGAZINE: WESTWARD

**54**
ARTIST: **JACK UNRUH**    ART DIRECTOR: HARVEY GRUT    MAGAZINE: SPORTS ILLUSTRATED

**55**
ARTIST: **RICHARD SCHLECHT**
ART DIRECTOR: JAN ADKINS
MAGAZINE: NATIONAL GEOGRAPHIC

**56**
ARTIST: **ALDRYTH OCKENGA**
ART DIRECTOR: ALDRYTH OCKENGA
MAGAZINE: CITY GUIDE

**BRALDT BRALDS**    ART DIRECTOR: ROGER CARPENTER    MAGAZINE: RADIO-EYES

**58**

ARTIST: **BRAD HOLLAND**

ART DIRECTOR: BOB CIANO
MAGAZINE: LIFE

**59**

ARTIST: **MICK HAGGERTY**

ART DIRECTOR: LLOYD ZIFF
MAGAZINE: VANITY FAIR

**60**
ARTIST: **ROBERT RISKO**
ART DIRECTOR: LLOYD ZIFF
MAGAZINE: VANITY FAIR

**61**
ARTIST: **STEVEN KELEMEN**
ART DIRECTOR: LLOYD ZIFF
MAGAZINE: VANITY FAIR

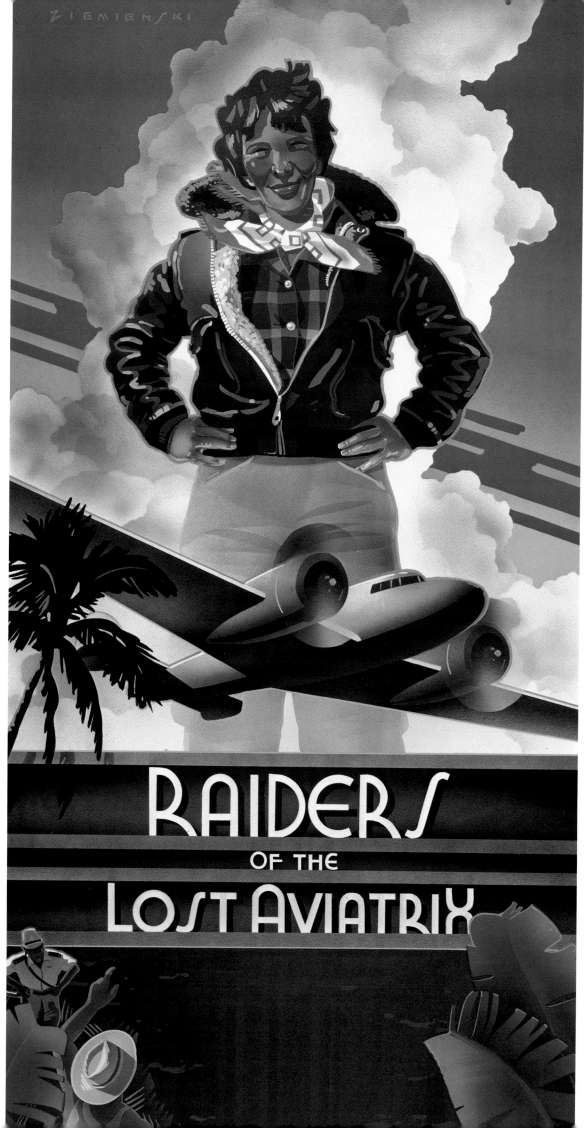

62
ARTIST: **DENNIS ZIEMIENSKI**
ART DIRECTOR: GREG PAUL
MAGAZINE: CLEVELAND PLAIN DEALER

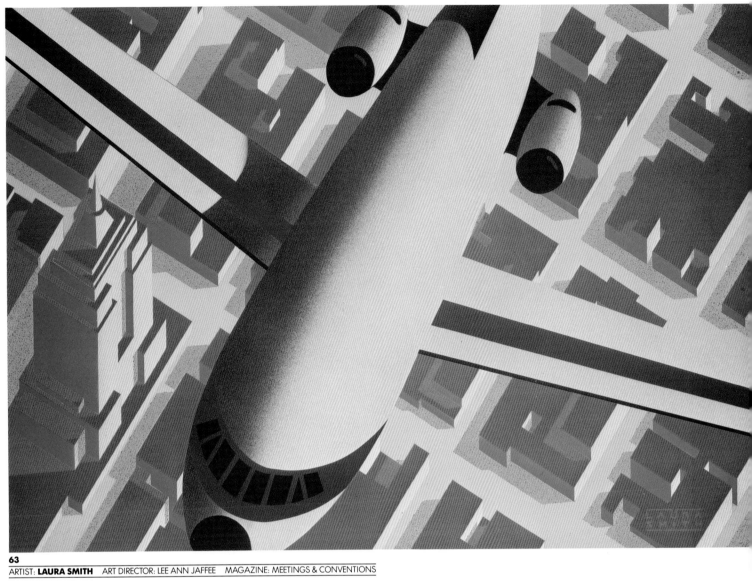

63
ARTIST: **LAURA SMITH**   ART DIRECTOR: LEE ANN JAFFEE   MAGAZINE: MEETINGS & CONVENTIONS

64
ARTIST: **DENNIS ZIEMIENSKI**   ART DIRECTOR: GREG PAUL   MAGAZINE: CLEVELAND PLAIN DEALER

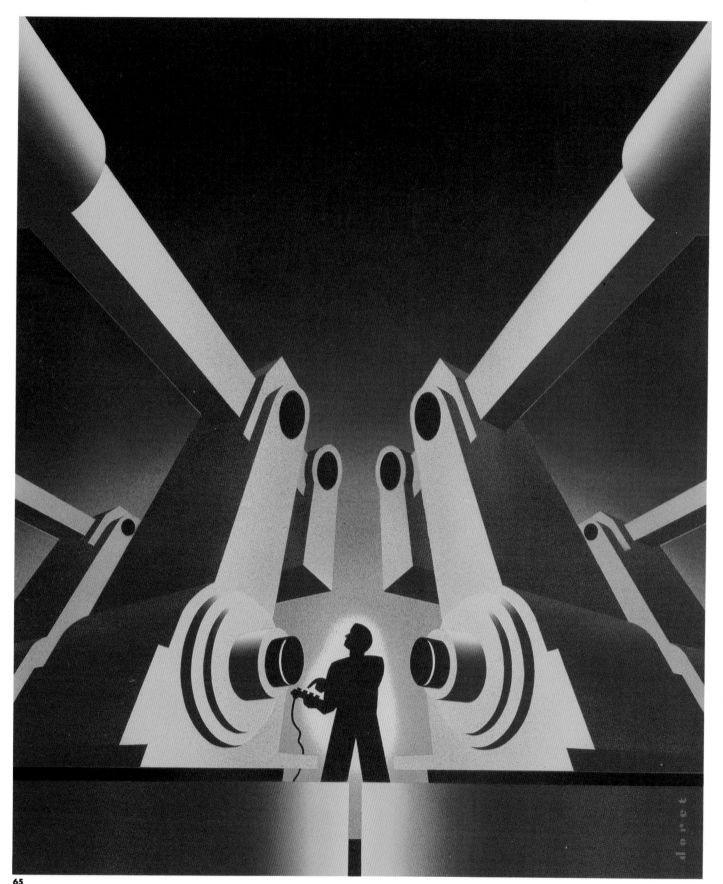

65
ARTIST: **MICHAEL DORET**
ART DIRECTOR: MARGERY PETERS
MAGAZINE: FORTUNE

66
ARTIST: **DAVE CALVER**
ART DIRECTOR: ROBERT BEST/PATRICIA BRADBURY
MAGAZINE: NEW YORK

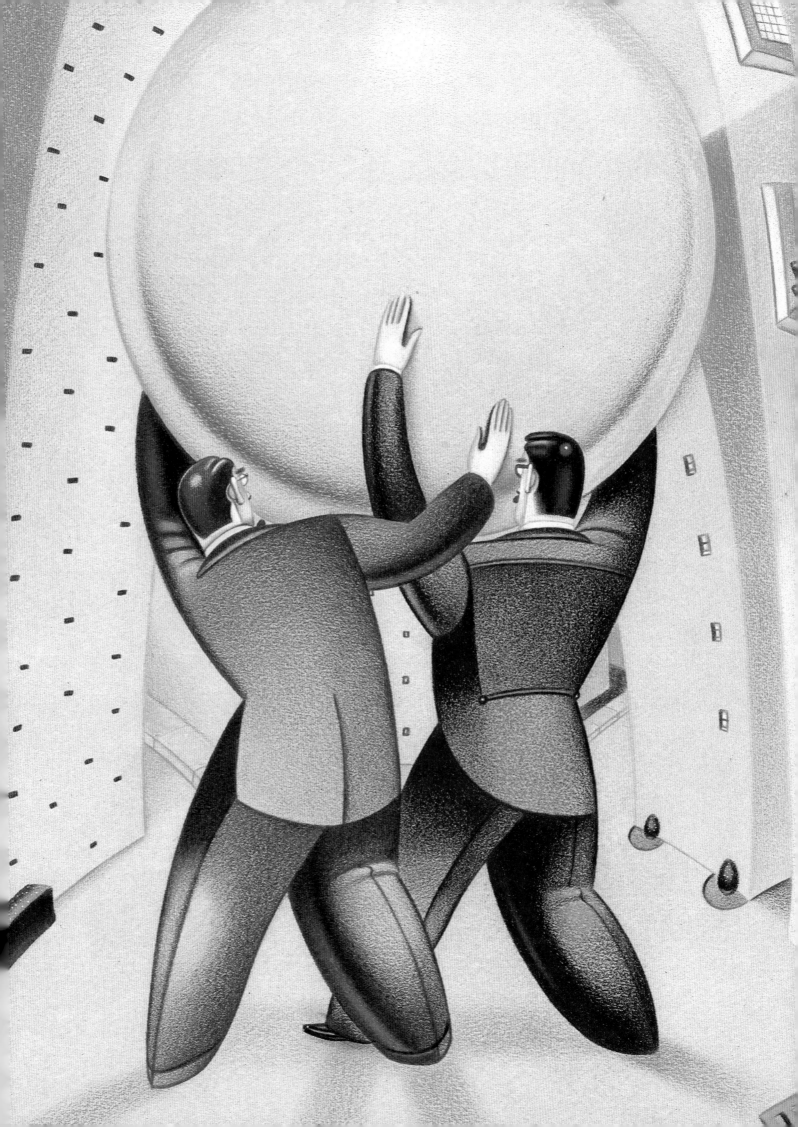

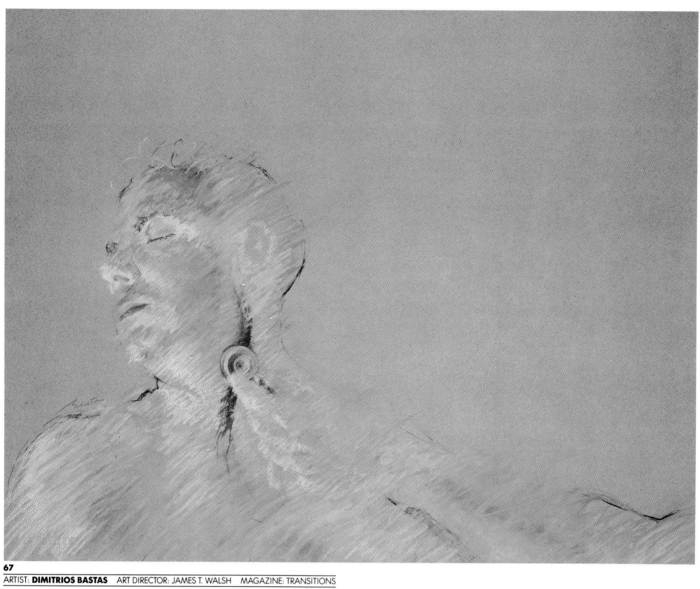

**67**
ARTIST: **DIMITRIOS BASTAS**    ART DIRECTOR: JAMES T. WALSH    MAGAZINE: TRANSITIONS

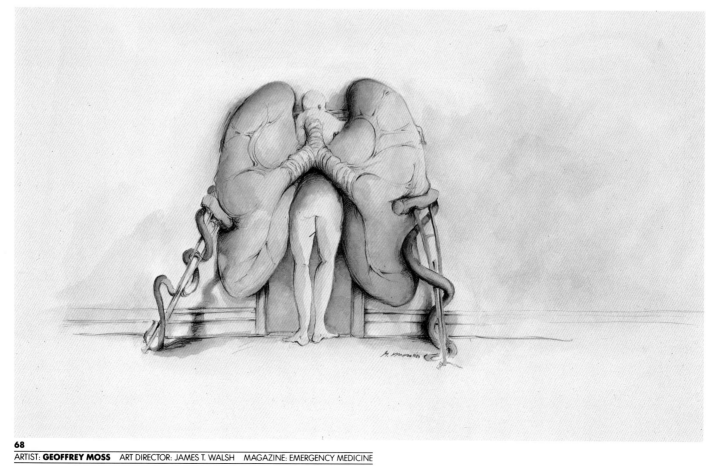

**68**
ARTIST: **GEOFFREY MOSS**    ART DIRECTOR: JAMES T. WALSH    MAGAZINE: EMERGENCY MEDICINE

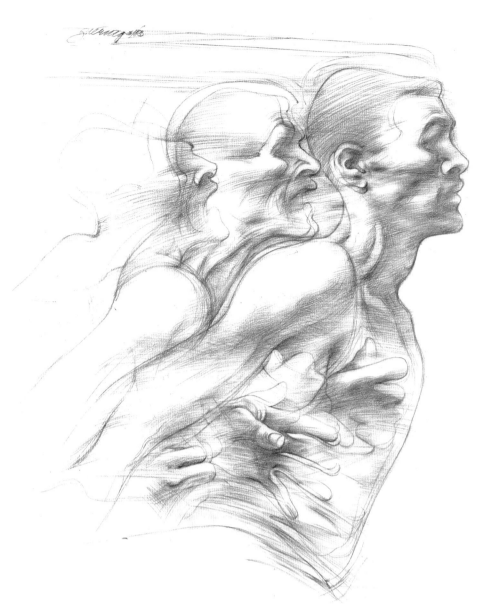

**69**
ARTIST: **BOB ZIERING**
ART DIRECTOR: RITA MILOS
MAGAZINE: THE RUNNER

**70**
ARTIST: **RANDALL ENOS**
ART DIRECTOR: BARBARA GROENTEMAN/JOHN NEWCOMB
MAGAZINE: MEDICAL ECONOMICS

**71**
ARTIST: **VINCENT NASTA**

**72**
ARTIST: **RICHARD SPARKS**
ART DIRECTOR: JOE CONNOLLY
MAGAZINE: BOY SCOUTS OF AMERICA

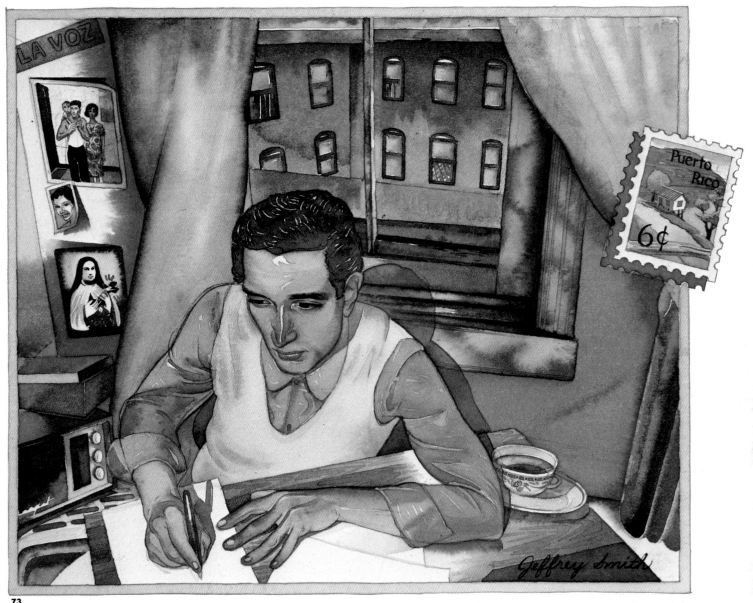

**73**

ARTIST: **JEFFREY J. SMITH**

ART DIRECTOR: THOMAS RUIS
MAGAZINE: NEW YORK DAILY NEWS

Margaret Cusack

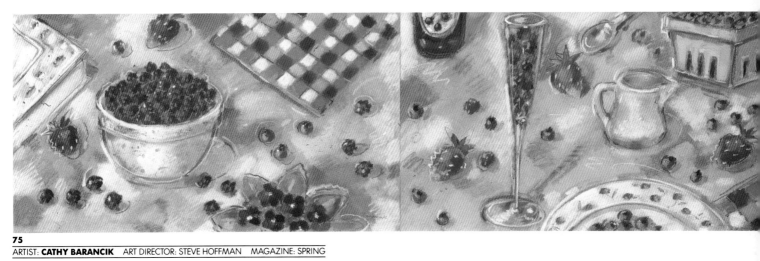

75
ARTIST: **CATHY BARANCIK**   ART DIRECTOR: STEVE HOFFMAN   MAGAZINE: SPRING

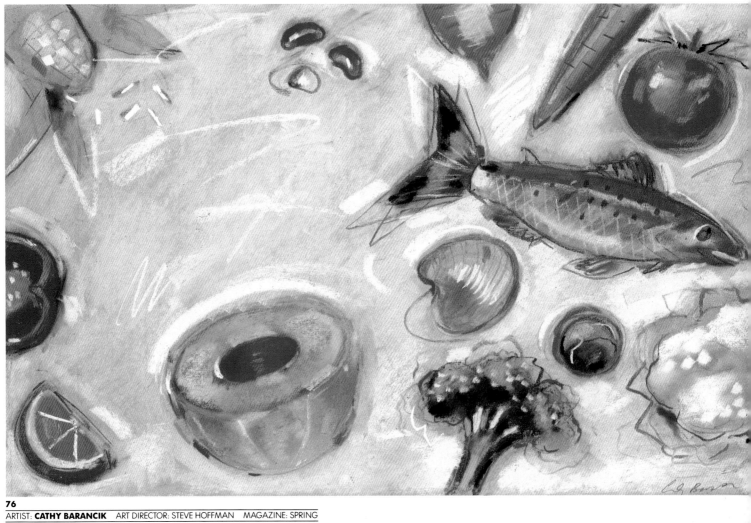

76
ARTIST: **CATHY BARANCIK**   ART DIRECTOR: STEVE HOFFMAN   MAGAZINE: SPRING

74
ARTIST: **MARGARET CUSACK**

ART DIRECTOR: DONALD DUFFY
MAGAZINE: READER'S DIGEST

**77**

ARTIST: **ED SOYKA**

ART DIRECTOR: RUDOLPH HOGLUND/IRENE RAMP
MAGAZINE: TIME

**78**

ARTIST: **DAVID LEE CSICSKO**

ART DIRECTOR: ROBERT J. POST
MAGAZINE: CHICAGO

ARTIST: **LOU BROOKS**    ART DIRECTOR: ROBERT ALTEMUS    MAGAZINE: FAMILY WEEKLY

**80**
ARTIST: **EDWARD SOREL**
ART DIRECTOR: JUDY GARLAN
MAGAZINE: THE ATLANTIC MONTHLY

**81**
ARTIST: **DAN KIRK**
ART DIRECTOR: MICHAEL GROSSMAN
MAGAZINE: NATIONAL LAMPOON

**82**
ARTIST: **CATHY BARANCIK**

ART DIRECTOR: PATRICIA BRADBURY
MAGAZINE: NEW YORK

**83**
ARTIST: **DAVID LEVINE**

ART DIRECTOR: LLOYD ZIFF
MAGAZINE: VANITY FAIR

**84**
ARTIST: **BRAD HOLLAND**

ART DIRECTOR: KEN KENDRICK
MAGAZINE: THE NEW YORK TIMES

**85**
ARTIST: **MATT MAHURIN**

ART DIRECTOR: RUDOLPH HOGLUND/IRENE RAMP
MAGAZINE: TIME MAGAZINE

ARTIST: **KINUKO CRAFT**   ART DIRECTOR: ALFRED ZELCER   MAGAZINE: PHILADELPHIA

**87**

ARTIST: **EDWARD SOREL**

ART DIRECTOR: JUDY GARLAN

MAGAZINE: THE ATLANTIC MONTHLY

**88**
ARTIST: **LANCE JACKSON**
ART DIRECTOR: VERONIQUE VIENNE
MAGAZINE: SAN FRANCISCO

**89**
ARTIST: **FRANCIS JETTER**
ART DIRECTOR: TINA ADAMEK
MAGAZINE: POSTGRADUATE MEDICINE

**90**
ARTIST: **WILLIAM BUERGE**
ART DIRECTOR: CHARLES DICKENS PHILLIPS
MAGAZINE: MICRO DISCOVERY

**91**
ARTIST: **BRAD HOLLAND**
ART DIRECTOR: TOM LUNDE
MAGAZINE: NEWSWEEK

**92**
ARTIST: **MICHAEL DORET**
ART DIRECTOR: FRED WOODWARD
MAGAZINE: TEXAS MONTHLY

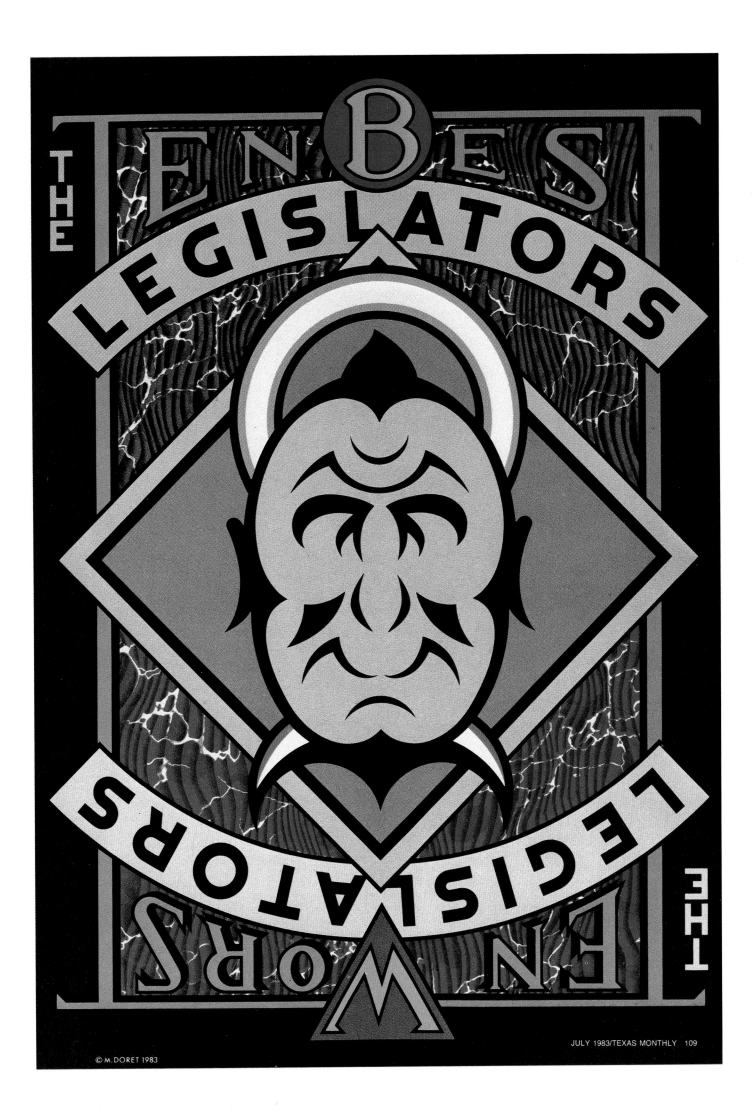

THE TEN BEST LEGISLATORS

THE TEN WORST LEGISLATORS

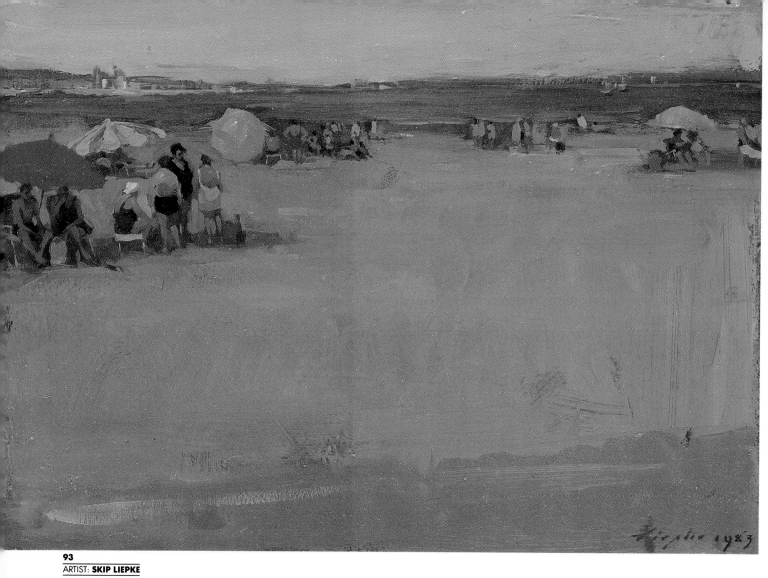

**93**
ARTIST: **SKIP LIEPKE**

**95**
ARTIST: **ROBERT HEINDEL**
ART DIRECTOR: HARVEY GRUT
MAGAZINE: SPORTS ILLUSTRATED

ARTIST: **DON VANDERBEEK**   ART DIRECTOR: DON VANDERBEEK   CLIENT: DAYTON NEWSPAPERS INC.

**96**

ARTIST: **WILLIAM LOW**
ART DIRECTOR: THOMAS RUIS
MAGAZINE: NEW YORK DAILY NEWS

**97**

ARTIST: **CHRISTOPHER MAGADINI**
ART DIRECTOR: LAWRENCE A. LAUKHUF
MAGAZINE: GUIDEPOSTS

**99**
ARTIST: **BARBARA ERICKSEN**   ART DIRECTOR: BARBARA ERICKSEN   MAGAZINE: ODYSSEY

**100**
ARTIST: **BRALDT BRALDS**   ART DIRECTOR: JUDY GARLAN   MAGAZINE: THE ATLANTIC MONTHLY

**101**
ARTIST: **BRALDT BRALDS**    ART DIRECTOR: JUDY GARLAN    MAGAZINE: THE ATLANTIC MONTHLY

**102**
ARTIST: **LARRY WINBORG**    ART DIRECTOR: HARVEY GRUT    MAGAZINE: SPORTS ILLUSTRATED

**103**
ARTIST: **KINUKO CRAFT**
ART DIRECTOR: MELISSA TARDIFF
MAGAZINE: TOWN & COUNTRY

**: SKIP LIEPKE**
RECTOR: MICHAEL ANDALORD
ZINE: NEW COVENANT

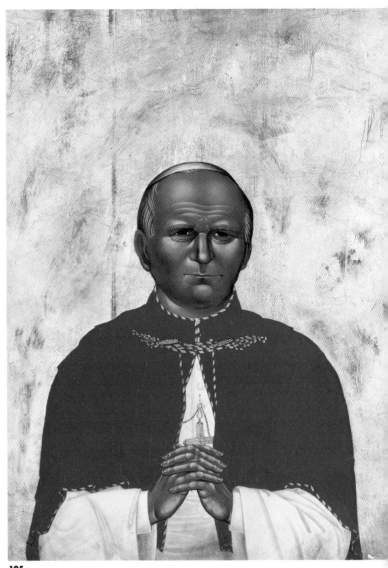

**105**
ARTIST: **KINUKO CRAFT**
ART DIRECTOR: RUDOLPH HOGLUND
MAGAZINE: TIME

**106**
ARTIST: **ALAN REINGOLD**
ART DIRECTOR: EVERETT HALVORSEN/ROGER ZAPKE
MAGAZINE: FORBES

**107**
ARTIST: **AL BRANDTNER**
ART DIRECTOR: CHARLES AURINGER
MAGAZINE: VIDIOT

**108**
ARTIST: **RICK TULKA**
ART DIRECTOR: CATHY CACCHIONE
MAGAZINE: AUDIO

**109**
ARTIST: **THOMAS WOODRUFF**
ART DIRECTOR: FRED WOODWARD
MAGAZINE: TEXAS MONTHLY

110
ARTIST: **JOHN COLLIER**    ART DIRECTOR: TINA ADAMEK    MAGAZINE: POSTGRADUATE MEDICINE

A SNORKLE, A MASK AND SWIM FINS MAKE A GOOD SWIMMER INTO AN UNDERWATER EXPLORER.

# SKIN DIVING SCOUTS

BY RICHARD WEISSMANN
Illustrated by Bob Dacey

**111**
ARTIST: **BOB DACEY**
ART DIRECTOR: JOE CONNOLLY
MAGAZINE: BOY'S LIFE

**112**
ARTIST: **SHARON DRINKWINE**
ART DIRECTOR: STAN McCRAY
MAGAZINE: BOSTON

**113**
ARTIST: **ELWOOD H. SMITH**
ART DIRECTOR: JOHN TWOHEY
MAGAZINE: CHICAGO TRIBUNE

**114**
ARTIST: **TOM McFARLAND**
ART DIRECTOR: TOM McFARLAND
CLIENT: RALSTON PURINA

**115**
ARTIST: **RANDALL ENOS**
ART DIRECTOR: JOE CONNOLLY
MAGAZINE: BOY'S LIFE

**116**
ARTIST: **FRANK MORRIS**
ART DIRECTOR: JOE CONNOLLY
MAGAZINE: BOY'S LIFE

**117**
ARTIST: **LAURA SMITH**
ART DIRECTOR: LEE ANN JAFFEE
MAGAZINE: MEETINGS & CONVENTIONS

**118**
ARTIST: **GUY BILLOUT**
ART DIRECTOR: JUDY GARLAN
MAGAZINE: THE ATLANTIC MONTHLY

ARTIST: **LAURA SMITH**    ART DIRECTOR: LEE ANN JAFFEE    MAGAZINE: MEETINGS & CONVENTIONS

**120**
ARTIST: **DENNIS LUZAK**
ART DIRECTOR: HARVEY GRUT
MAGAZINE: SPORTS ILLUSTRATED

**121**
ARTIST: **RICHARD SPARKS**
ART DIRECTOR: HARVEY GRUT
MAGAZINE: SPORTS ILLUSTRATED

**122**
ARTIST: **DENNIS LUZAK**
ART DIRECTOR: HARVEY GRUT
MAGAZINE: SPORTS ILLUSTRATED

**123**
ARTIST: **DAVID NOYES**
ART DIRECTOR: ALFRED ZELCER
MAGAZINE: PHILADELPHIA

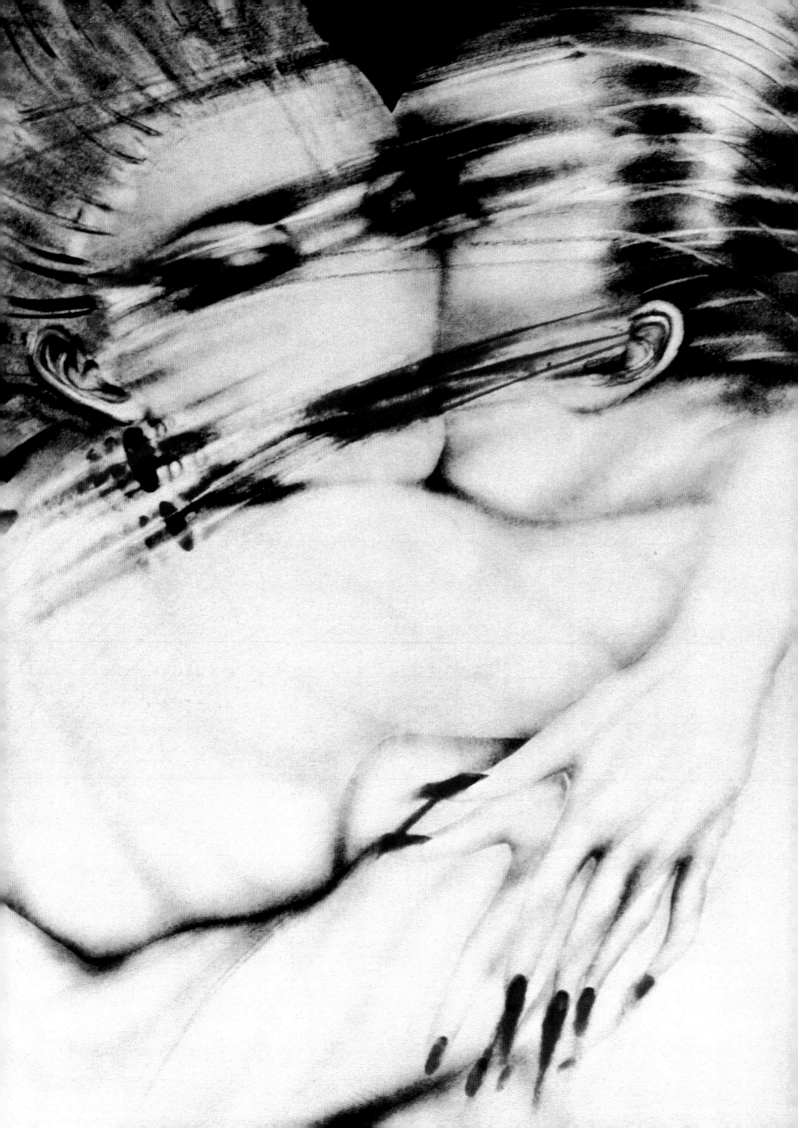

**125**
ARTIST: **GEOFFREY GEARY**
ART DIRECTOR: BRUCE DANBROT
MAGAZINE: GOOD HOUSEKEEPING

**126**
ARTIST: **BOB DACEY**
ART DIRECTOR: TAMARA SNEIDER
MAGAZINE: LADIES' HOME JOURNAL

AN OLD, SWEET LOVE

**124**
ARTIST: **MARZENA KAWALEROWICZ**
ART DIRECTOR: TOM STAEBLER/KERIG POPE
MAGAZINE: PLAYBOY

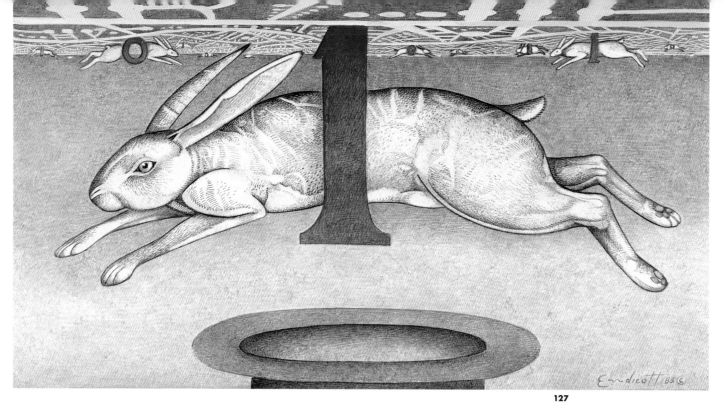

**127**
ARTIST: **JIM ENDICOTT**
ART DIRECTOR: CHARLES DICKENS PHILLIPS
MAGAZINE: MICRO DISCOVERY

**128**
ARTIST: **MILTON GLASER**
ART DIRECTOR: TOM STAEBLER/KERIG POPE
MAGAZINE: PLAYBOY

# JURY

**GERRY GERSTEN,** CHAIRMAN

Freelance illustrator and caricaturist for advertising, magazines, books and television.

**JEFF CORNELL**

Freelance illustrator, exhibited at the Society of Illustrators and AIGA.

**ROBERT DESCHAMPS**

Freelance illustrator. Awards from Art Directors Club, ANDY and *Communication Arts.*

**GEORGE LAMBOS**

Art Director, Cato Johnson/ Young & Rubicam.

**BENNETT ROBINSON**

Chairman of Corporate Graphics, Inc. Instructor at Pratt Institute, Awards from AIGA, Andy, *Graphis, Communication Arts,* the Society of Illustrators.

**BARRY ROSS**

Freelance illustrator for advertising, magazine and promotion.

**WALT SPITZMILLER**

Freelance illustrator, one-man shows in New York, the Southwest and Canada.

**STEPHEN TARANTAL**

Freelance illustrator/designer. Professor, Illustration Department, Philadelphia College of Art. Awards from the Society and Art Directors Club of New York.

**CAROL WALD**

Illustrator/painter/author. Gold medal winner, Society of Illustrators. Work in the collections of the Museum of Art, St. Paul; The National Gallery and Detroit Institute of Arts.

# BOOK

**130**

ARTIST: **SKIP LIEPKE**    ART DIRECTOR: CHRIS MORRIS/JANET TAGGART    PUBLISHER: CORONADO

**GOLD MEDAL**

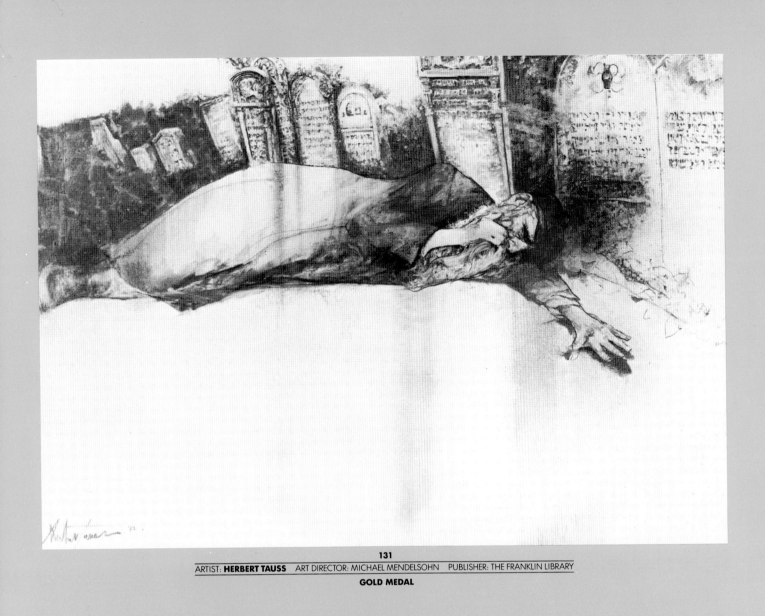

**131**

ARTIST: **HERBERT TAUSS**   ART DIRECTOR: MICHAEL MENDELSOHN   PUBLISHER: THE FRANKLIN LIBRARY

**GOLD MEDAL**

**132**

ARTIST: **VIVIENNE FLESHER**    ART DIRECTOR: LARRY KAZAL    PUBLISHER: WILLIAM MORROW & COMPANY

**GOLD MEDAL**

133

ARTIST: **MICHAEL DAVID BROWN**    ART DIRECTOR: MICHAEL DAVID BROWN    PUBLISHER: OUTLOOK REVIEW

**SILVER MEDAL**

**134**

ARTIST: **JEANNE TITHERINGTON**     ART DIRECTOR: WILLIAM F. LUCKEY/SARAH SAINT-ONGE     PUBLISHER: DAVID R. GODINE

**SILVER MEDAL**

135

ARTIST: **CHRIS VAN ALLSBURG**    ART DIRECTOR: SUSAN SHERMAN    PUBLISHER: HOUGHTON-MIFFLIN

**SILVER MEDAL**

**136**

ARTIST: **LEO & DIANE DILLON**

ART DIRECTOR: BARBARA G. HENNESSY
PUBLISHER: VIKING PENGUIN, INC.

ST: **RICHARD SPARKS**
DIRECTOR: ANGELO PERRONE
ISHER: READER'S DIGEST

**138**
ARTIST: **RICHARD SPARKS**
ART DIRECTOR: ANGELO PERRONE
PUBLISHER: READER'S DIGEST

**139**
ARTIST: **PAUL GIOVANOPOULOS**
ART DIRECTOR: DON MUNSON
PUBLISHER: BALLANTINE BOOKS

**140**
ARTIST: **MING XIAN CHEN**

ARTIST: **MARGARET CUSACK**    ART DIRECTOR: RUBIN PFEFFER    PUBLISHER: HARCOURT BRACE JOVANOVICH

ARTIST: **MARK ENGLISH**   ART DIRECTOR: MATT TEPPER   PUBLISHER: AVON BOOKS

**143**
ARTIST: **CAROL WALD**
ART DIRECTOR: BOB MITCHELL
PUBLISHER: McGRAW HILL

**144**
ARTIST: **JEFF CORNELL**
ART DIRECTOR: MARION DAVIS
MAGAZINE: READER'S DIGEST

**145**
ARTIST: **SKIP LIEPKE**
ART DIRECTOR: CHRIS MORRIS/JANET TAGGART
PUBLISHER: CORONADO

**146**
ARTIST: **ELAINE RAPHAEL/DON BOLOGNES**
ART DIRECTOR: MICHAEL MENDELSOHN
PUBLISHER: THE FRANKLIN LIBRARY

**147**
ARTIST: **IVAN POWELL**
ART DIRECTOR: CHRIS PETERSON/JESSICA WEBER
PUBLISHER: BOOK OF THE MONTH CLUB

**148**
ARTIST: **HERBERT TAUSS**
ART DIRECTOR: MICHAEL MENDELSOHN
PUBLISHER: THE FRANKLIN LIBRARY

**150**
ARTIST: **ARNOLD LOBEL**
ART DIRECTOR: CATHY GOLDSMITH
PUBLISHER: RANDOM HOUSE

**151**
ARTIST: **JACK STOCKMAN**
PUBLISHER: DAVID C. COOK

**149**
ARTIST: **GUY BILLOUT**
ART DIRECTOR: BARBARA FRANCIS
PUBLISHER: PRENTICE-HALL

ARTIST: **FRISO HENSTRA**   ART DIRECTOR: TOM VONDERLINN   PUBLISHER: READER'S DIGEST

**153**
ARTIST: **RICHARD EGIELSKI**
ART DIRECTOR: MICHAEL DICAPUA
PUBLISHER: FARRAR, STRAUS & GIROUX

**154**
ARTIST: **RICHARD EGIELSKI**
ART DIRECTOR: MICHAEL DICAPUA
PUBLISHER: FARRAR, STRAUS & GIROUX

**155**
ARTIST: **BOB RADIGAN**
ART DIRECTOR: BOB RADIGAN
PUBLISHER: FOLLETT LIBRARY BOOK CO.

**156**
ARTIST: **HODGES SOILEAU**
ART DIRECTOR: CHRIS MORRIS/JANET TAGGART
PUBLISHER: CORONADO

**157**
ARTIST: **BOB DACEY**
ART DIRECTOR: CHRIS MORRIS/JANET TAGGART
PUBLISHER: CORONADO

**158**
ARTIST: **BURT SILVERMAN**
ART DIRECTOR: CHRIS MORRIS/JANET TAGGART
PUBLISHER: CORONADO

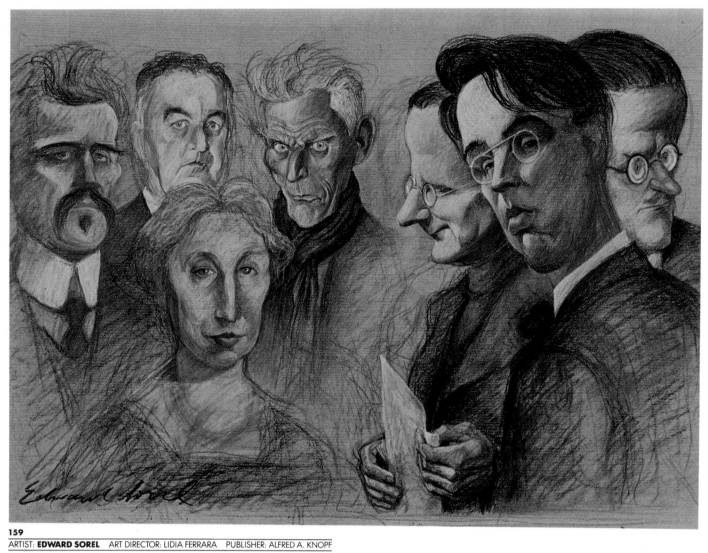

**159**
ARTIST: **EDWARD SOREL**    ART DIRECTOR: LIDIA FERRARA    PUBLISHER: ALFRED A. KNOPF

**160**
ARTIST: **RICK McCOLLUM**
ART DIRECTOR: CHRIS MORRIS/JANET TAGGART
PUBLISHER: CORONADO

**161**
ARTIST: **HODGES SOILEAU**
ART DIRECTOR: RICH CARTER
PUBLISHER: EASTON PRESS

**162**
ARTIST: **BOB BARANCIK**
ART DIRECTOR: AMY BLAKE
PUBLISHER: NEW PENN PRESS

**163**
ARTIST: **MADELAINE GILL LINDEN**
ART DIRECTOR: BARBARA FENTON
PUBLISHER: THOMAS Y. CROWELL

**164**

ARTIST: **LEONARD BASKIN**
ART DIRECTOR: DENISE CRONIN
PUBLISHER: KNOPF/PANTHEON BOOKS FOR YOUNG READERS

**165**
ARTIST: **ANN MEISEL**    ART DIRECTOR: FRANK KOZELEK/GENE MYDLOWSKI    PUBLISHER: BERKLEY BOOKS

**166**
ARTIST: **HERBERT TAUSS**
ART DIRECTOR: MICHAEL MENDELSOHN
PUBLISHER: THE FRANKLIN LIBRARY

**167**
ARTIST: **BRIAN FROUD**
ART DIRECTOR: JACKIE MERRI MEYER
PUBLISHER: MACMILLAN GENERAL BOOKS

168
ARTIST: **MICHAEL WHELAN**
ART DIRECTOR: DON MUNSON
PUBLISHER: BALLANTINE BOOKS

169
ARTIST: **JOHN THOMPSON**
ART DIRECTOR: MARION DAVIS
PUBLISHER: READER'S DIGEST

**170**
ARTIST: **NORMAN WALKER**
ART DIRECTOR: MATT TEPPER
PUBLISHER: AVON BOOKS

**171**
ARTIST: **GUY BILLOUT**
ART DIRECTOR: BARBARA FRANCIS
PUBLISHER: PRENTICE-HALL

**172**
ARTIST: **JILL BAUMAN**

**173**
ARTIST: **ZEVI BLUM**

ART DIRECTOR: MICHAEL MENDELSOHN
PUBLISHER: THE FRANKLIN LIBRARY

**174**
ARTIST: **RICK McCOLLUM**
ART DIRECTOR: CHRIS MORRIS/JANET TAGGART
PUBLISHER: CORONADO

**175**
ARTIST: **LEO LIONNI**    ART DIRECTOR: DENISE CRONIN    PUBLISHER: KNOPF/PANTHEON BOOKS FOR YOUNG READERS

**176**
ARTIST: **LEO LIONNI**    ART DIRECTOR: DENISE CRONIN    PUBLISHER: KNOPF/PANTHEON BOOKS FOR YOUNG READERS

ARTIST: **LEONARD BASKIN**   ART DIRECTOR: DENISE CRONIN   PUBLISHER: KNOPF/PANTHEON BOOKS FOR YOUNG READERS

178
ARTIST: **BERNIE FUCHS**
ART DIRECTOR: ISKA ROTHOVIUS
PUBLISHER: NEW YORK TELEPHONE COMPANY

**179**
ARTIST: **MAX GINSBURG**
ART DIRECTOR: LEN LEONE
PUBLISHER: BANTAM BOOKS

**180**
ARTIST: **SEYMOUR CHWAST**
ART DIRECTOR: BARBARA G. HENNESSY
PUBLISHER: VIKING PENGUIN, INC.

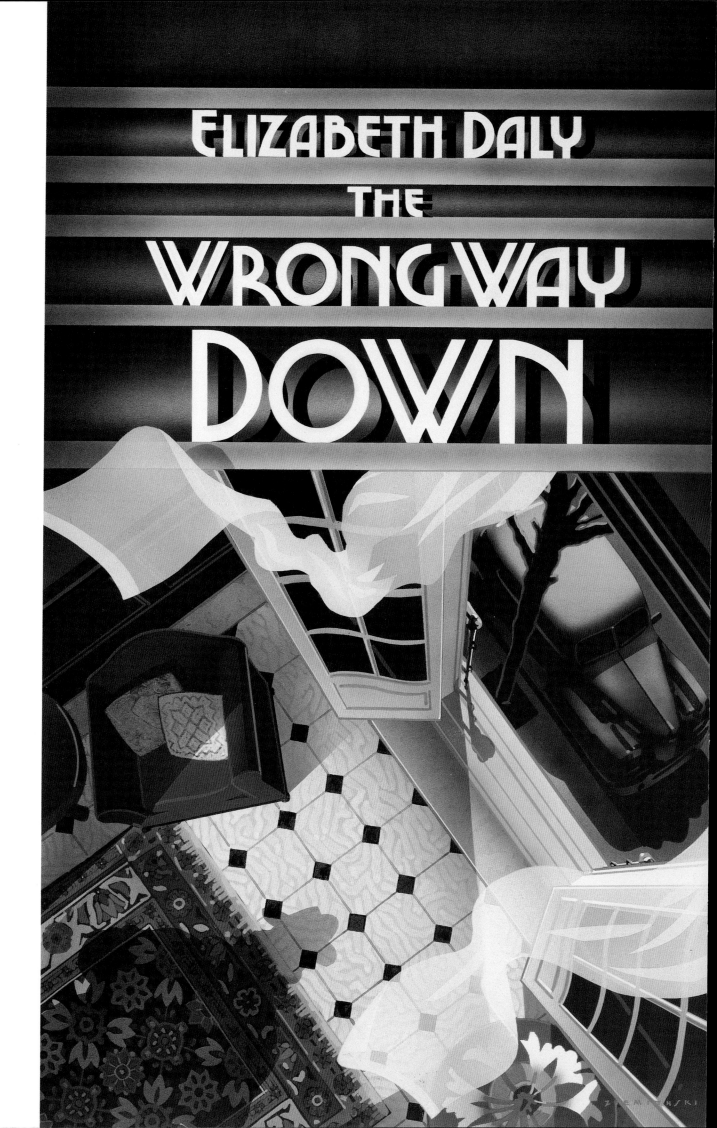

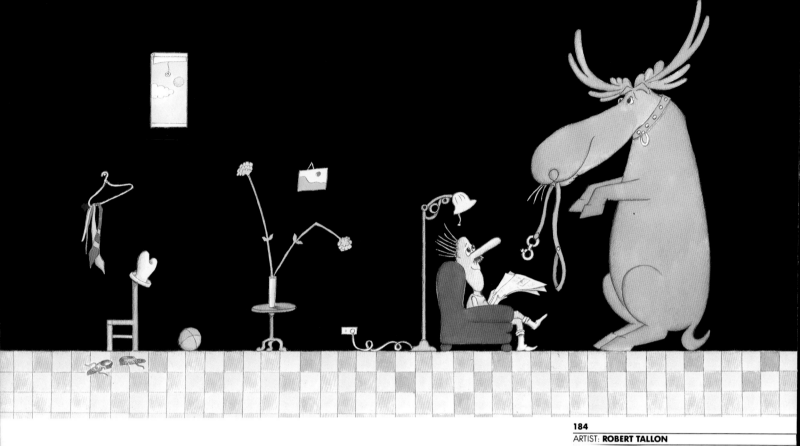

**184**

ARTIST: **ROBERT TALLON**

ART DIRECTOR: DENISE CRONIN

PUBLISHER: KNOPF/PANTHEON BOOKS FOR YOUNG READERS

**185**

ARTIST: **MICHAEL DEAS**

ART DIRECTOR: LEN LEONE

PUBLISHER: BANTAM BOOKS

**186**
ARTIST: **TOMIE dePAOLA**    ART DIRECTOR: DAVID ROGERS    PUBLISHER: HOLIDAY HOUSE

**187**
ARTIST: **FRISO HENSTRA**    ART DIRECTOR: TOM VONDERLINN    PUBLISHER: READER'S DIGEST

**188**
ARTIST: **DAVID MACAULAY**
ART DIRECTOR: SUSAN SHERMAN
PUBLISHER: HOUGHTON-MIFFLIN

**189**
ARTIST: **HARRY BLISS**
ART DIRECTOR: J. ROBERT TERINGO
PUBLISHER: NATIONAL GEOGRAPHIC SOCIETY

190
ARTIST: **DAVID JEMERSON YOUNG**     ART DIRECTOR: GREGG BUTLER     PUBLISHER: BOBBS-MERRILL CO., INC.

**191**

ARTIST: **DAVID MONTIEL**

ART DIRECTOR: LOUISE FILI
PUBLISHER: PANTHEON BOOKS

**192**

ARTIST: **DANIEL SCHWARTZ**

ART DIRECTOR: ARNOLD SCHWARTZMAN
PUBLISHER: SIMON WIESENTHAL CENTER FOR HOLOCAUST STUDIES

**193**

ARTIST: **PAUL DAVIS**

ART DIRECTOR: PAUL DAVIS
PUBLISHER: CLARKSON N. POTTER, INC.

ARTIST: **VINCENT NASTA**    ART DIRECTOR: ROBERT GIUSTI

**195**
ARTIST: **VIVIENNE FLESHER**
ART DIRECTOR: LARRY KAZAL
PUBLISHER: WILLIAM MORROW & COMPANY

GORGEOUS·VII· ANNO·1983·

**196**
ARTIST: **BRALDT BRALDS**
ART DIRECTOR: PIET VAN OSS
PUBLISHER: LIBELLE

**197**
ARTIST: **SEYMOUR CHWAST**
ART DIRECTOR: SHELLEY WILLIAMS/DEBBIE SMITH
PUBLISHER: PET INFORMATION CENTER

**198**

ARTIST: **TOM HALL**

ART DIRECTOR: DON MUNSON
PUBLISHER: BALLANTINE BOOKS

**199**
ARTIST: **CHRIS VAN ALLSBURG**
ART DIRECTOR: SUSAN SHERMAN
PUBLISHER: HOUGHTON-MIFFLIN

**200**
ARTIST: **NITA ENGLE**
ART DIRECTOR: MARION DAVIS
PUBLISHER: READER'S DIGEST

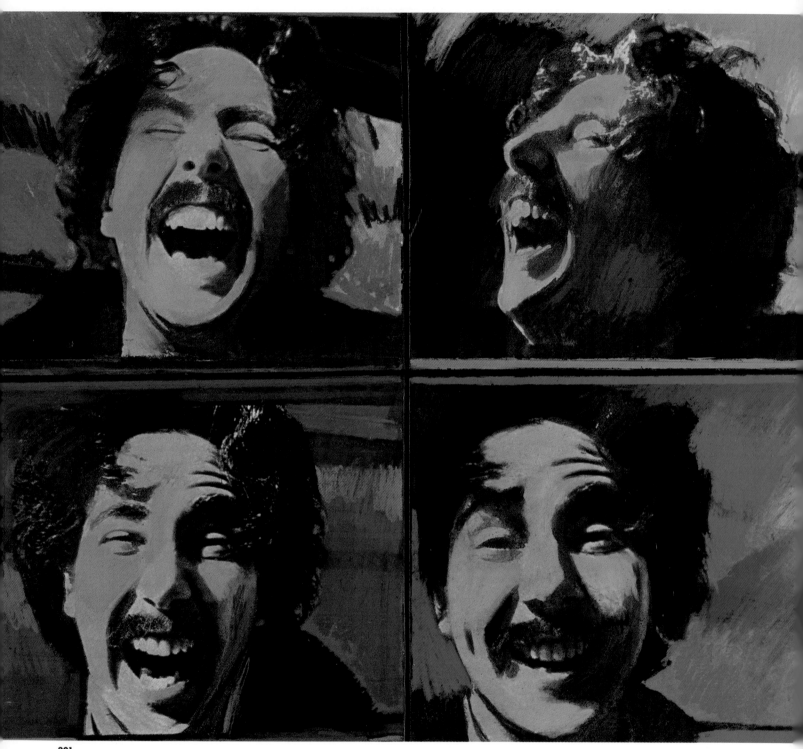

**201**
ARTIST: **JANE STERRETT**
ART DIRECTOR: ZLATA PACES/AVIS LARSON
PUBLISHER: MACMILLAN

MARK ROTHKO     VAN HOWELL

**202**

ARTIST: **VAN HOWELL**

ART DIRECTOR: ROGER HUBBARD
PUBLISHER: GALE RESEARCH COMPANY

**204**

ARTIST: **NEIL WALDMAN**

ART DIRECTOR: CONNIE FTERA
PUBLISHER: PRENTICE-HALL

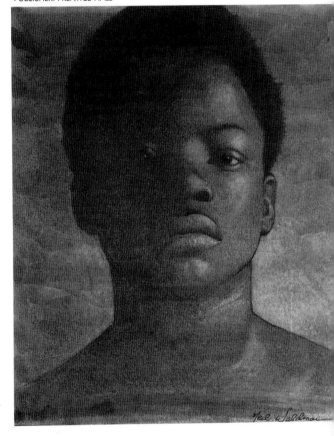

**203**

ARTIST: **HODGES SOILEAU**

ART DIRECTOR: ANGELO PERRONE
PUBLISHER: READER'S DIGEST

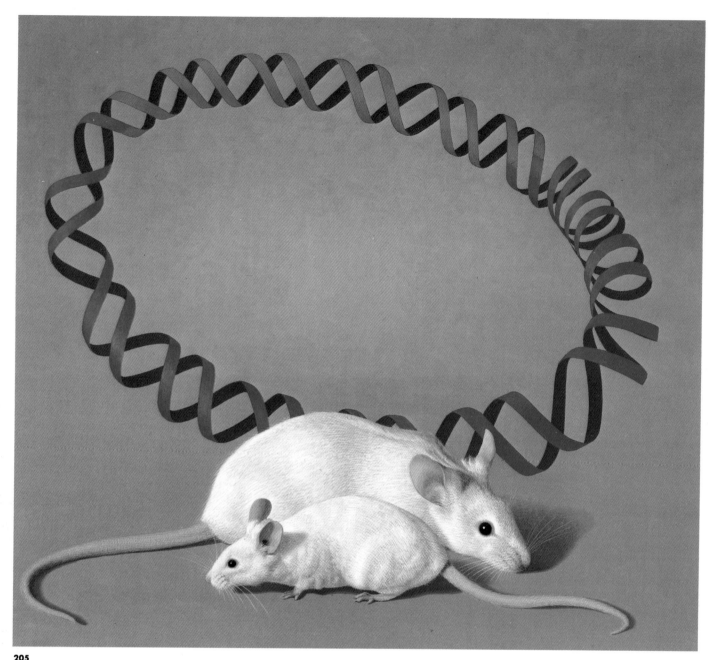

**205**
ARTIST: **MARVIN MATTELSON**   ART DIRECTOR: LINN FISCHER   PUBLISHER: SCIENTIFIC AMERICAN BOOKS

**206**
ARTIST: **ROBERT JOHN BYRD**   ART DIRECTOR: RIKI LEVINSON   PUBLISHER: E.P. DUTTON

207
ARTIST: **SCOTT REYNOLDS**

208
ARTIST: **ALICE & MARTIN PROVENSEN**
ART DIRECTOR: BARBARA G. HENNESSY
PUBLISHER: VIKING PENGUIN, INC.

**209**
ARTIST: **RICHARD HARVEY**    ART DIRECTOR: WILLIAM GREGORY    PUBLISHER: READER'S DIGEST

**210**
ARTIST: **CHRISTOPHER BLOSSOM**    ART DIRECTOR: ANGELO PERRONE    PUBLISHER: READER'S DIGEST

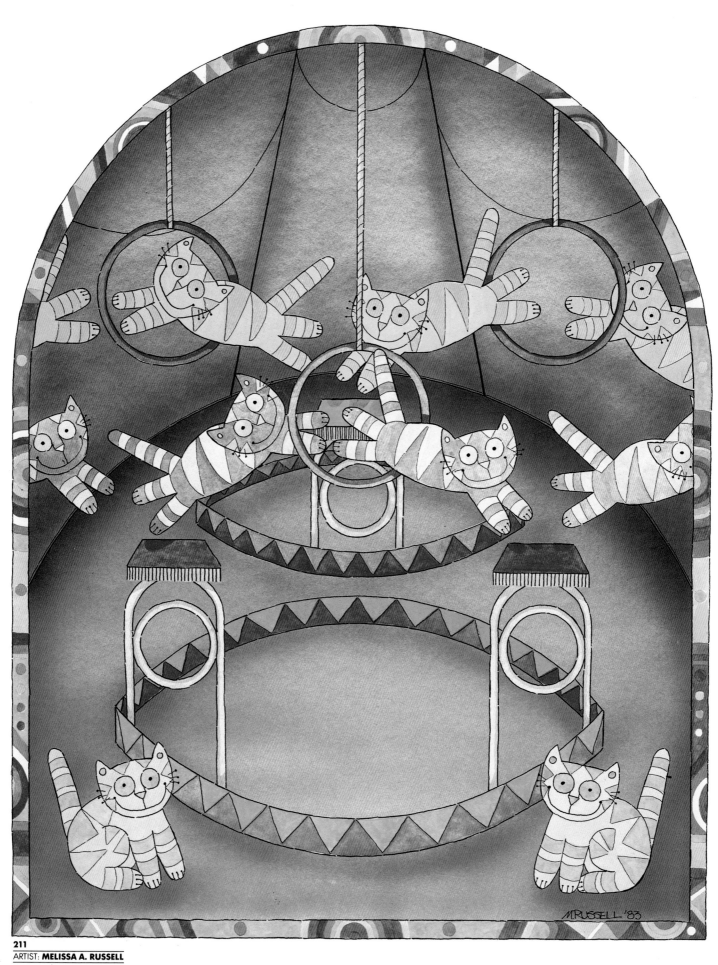

ARTIST: **MELISSA A. RUSSELL**

**212**
ARTIST: **TAK MURAKAMI**
ART DIRECTOR: GLORIA J. MUCZYNSKI
PUBLISHER: LAIDLAW BROTHERS

**213**
ARTIST: **MICHAEL WHELAN**
ART DIRECTOR: MICHAEL WHELAN
PUBLISHER: TOR BOOKS

**214**
ARTIST: **FRISO HENSTRA**    ART DIRECTOR: TOM VONDERLINN    PUBLISHER: READER'S DIGEST

**215**
ARTIST: **SUSAN KILGORE**
PUBLISHER: SYNERGISTIC ASSOCIATES

**216**
ARTIST: **CHARLES REID**
ART DIRECTOR: SOREN NORING
PUBLISHER: READER'S DIGEST

**220**
ARTIST: **JOE D'ESPOSITO**

**217**
ARTIST: **ROBERT HEINDEL**
ART DIRECTOR: MILTON CHARLES
PUBLISHER: POCKET BOOKS

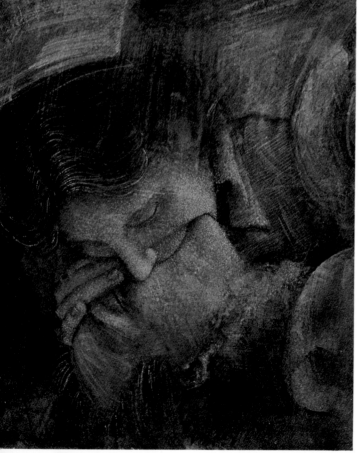

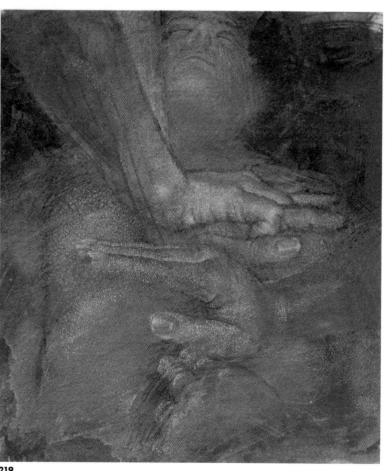

**218**
ARTIST: **DAVID CHRISTIANA**
ART DIRECTOR: LISA GILDE

**219**
ARTIST: **DAVID CHRISTIANA**
ART DIRECTOR: LISA GILDE

**221**

ARTIST: **JAY MATTERNES**    ART DIRECTOR: J. ROBERT TERINGO    PUBLISHER: NATIONAL GEOGRAPHIC SOCIETY

**222**

ARTIST: **ROBERT McGINNIS**    ART DIRECTOR: J. ROBERT TERINGO    PUBLISHER: NATIONAL GEOGRAPHIC SOCIETY

ARTIST: **BERNARD D'ANDREA**    ART DIRECTOR: J. ROBERT TERINGO    PUBLISHER: NATIONAL GEOGRAPHIC SOCIETY

**224**
ARTIST: **BOB LAPSLEY**

ART DIRECTOR: JIM PLUMERI
PUBLISHER: NEW AMERICAN LIBRARY

**225**
ARTIST: **PATRICIA HENDERSON LINCOLN**

ART DIRECTOR: MATT TEPPER
PUBLISHER: AVON BOOKS

**226**
ARTIST: **LISA FALKENSTERN**

ART DIRECTOR: MILTON CHARLES
PUBLISHER: POCKET BOOKS

**227**
ARTIST: **RANDALL McKISSICK**
ART DIRECTOR: TIM BOTT
PUBLISHER: TYNDALE HOUSE

**228**
ARTIST: **GLEN SMITH**
ART DIRECTOR: GLEN SMITH
PUBLISHER: SMITH & SMITH

229
ARTIST: **PATRICIA A. TOPPER**    ART DIRECTOR: DAVID M. SEAGER    PUBLISHER: NATIONAL GEOGRAPHIC SOCIETY

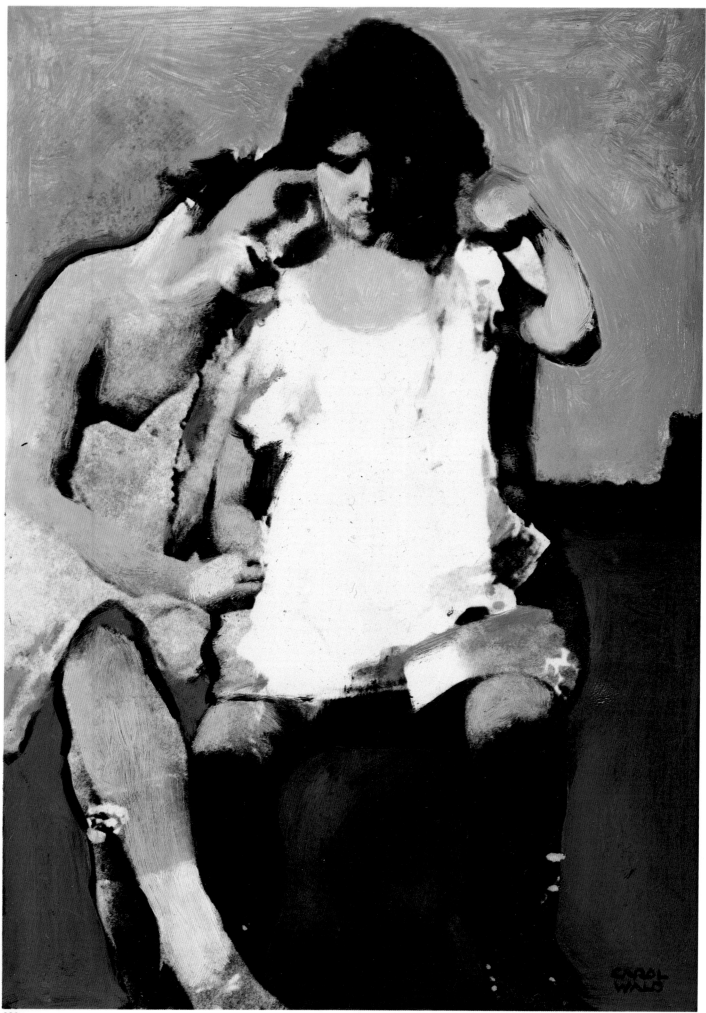

**230**
ARTIST: **CAROL WALD**

**231**
ARTIST: **PAUL HENRY**
ART DIRECTOR: SOREN NORING
PUBLISHER: READER'S DIGEST

**232**
ARTIST: **JILL DUBIN**
CLIENT: ROBYN FREEDMAN SPIZMAN

**233**
ARTIST: **LORI McELRATH-ESLICK**

**234**
ARTIST: **SUSAN SUMICHRAST**

**235**
ARTIST: **ROBERT M. CUNNINGHAM**

**237**

ARTIST: **FRED OTNES**

ART DIRECTOR: MICHAEL MENDELSOHN
PUBLISHER: THE FRANKLIN LIBRARY

**238**

ARTIST: **CARL METHFESSEL**

ART DIRECTOR: MATT TEPPER
PUBLISHER: AVON BOOKS

**236**

ARTIST: **FRED MARCELLINO**

ART DIRECTOR: LOUISE NOBLE
PUBLISHER: HOUGHTON-MIFFLIN

**239**
ARTIST: **ROBERT M. CUNNINGHAM**

**240**
ARTIST: **CHARLES ROBERT HOWE**
ART DIRECTOR: CHARLES ROBERT HOWE
CLIENT: THE C.V. MOSBY COMPANY

**241**
ARTIST: **DANIEL SCHWARTZ**    ART DIRECTOR: IVAN CHERMAYEFF    CLIENT: MOBIL OIL CORPORATION

**242**
ARTIST: **KAREN FARYNIAK**
CLIENT: COLOR SERVICES

**243**
ARTIST: **SKIP LIEPKE**

244
ARTIST: **CHARLES REID**
ART DIRECTOR: SOREN NORING
PUBLISHER: READER'S DIGEST

245
ARTIST: **RICHARD STEADHAM**
ART DIRECTOR: BYRON STEELE
PUBLISHER: BANNER BOOKS

**247**
ARTIST: **WENDELL MINOR**    ART DIRECTOR: LIDIA FERRARA    PUBLISHER: ALFRED A. KNOPF

**246**
ARTIST: **SUSAN KILGORE**
CLIENT: SYNERGISTIC ASSOCIATES

**249**
ARTIST: **BARRON STOREY**   ART DIRECTOR: MILTON CHARLES   PUBLISHER: POCKET BOOKS

**250**
ARTIST: **MICHAEL DAVID BROWN**
ART DIRECTOR: MICHAEL DAVID BROWN
PUBLISHER: OUTLOOK REVIEW

**251**
ARTIST: **MICHAEL DAVID BROWN**
ART DIRECTOR: MICHAEL DAVID BROWN
PUBLISHER: OUTLOOK REVIEW

**252**
ARTIST: **ED LINDLOF**
ART DIRECTOR: GEORGE LENOX
PUBLISHER: UNIVERSITY OF TEXAS PRESS

**253**
ARTIST: **JAMES HARVEY WILSON**

254
ARTIST: **MICHAEL DEAS**
ART DIRECTOR: JIM PLUMERI
PUBLISHER: NEW AMERICAN LIBRARY

255
ARTIST: **ROBERT McGINNIS**
ART DIRECTOR: FRANK KOZELEK
PUBLISHER: BERKLEY BOOKS

**256**
ARTIST: **JARMILA MARANOVA**
ART DIRECTOR: MICHAEL MENDELSOHN
PUBLISHER: THE FRANKLIN LIBRARY

**257**
ARTIST: **JARMILA MARANOVA**
ART DIRECTOR: MICHAEL MENDELSOHN
PUBLISHER: THE FRANKLIN LIBRARY

**258**
ARTIST: **JANUSZ KAPUSTA**
ART DIRECTOR: BEN SHIFF
PUBLISHER: THE LIMITED EDITION CLUB

**259**
ARTIST: **JOHN GURNEY**

**260**
ARTIST: **SUE ROTHER**
ART DIRECTOR: MARY MARS
PUBLISHER: SCHOLASTIC

**261**
ARTIST: **TRINA SCHART HYMAN**
ART DIRECTOR: DAVID ROGERS
PUBLISHER: HOLIDAY HOUSE

**262**
ARTIST: **SARA SCHWARTZ**

**263**
ARTIST: **JUDY PEDERSEN**   ART DIRECTOR: BOB AULICINO   PUBLISHER: PANTHEON BOOKS

**264**
ARTIST: **HERBERT TAUSS**
ART DIRECTOR: MICHAEL MENDELSOHN
PUBLISHER: THE FRANKLIN LIBRARY

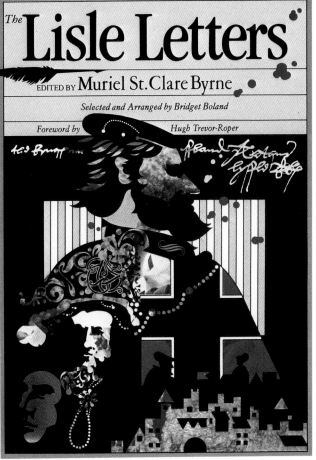

**265**
ARTIST: **MICHAEL DAVID BROWN**
ART DIRECTOR: CAMERON POULTER
PUBLISHER: UNIVERSITY OF CHICAGO PRESS

**266**

ARTIST: **BURT SILVERMAN**

ART DIRECTOR: CHRIS MORRIS/JANET TAGGART
PUBLISHER: CORONADO

**267**
ARTIST: **RICK McCOLLUM**
ART DIRECTOR: BOB SAIELLI
PUBLISHER: CORONADO

**268**
ARTIST: **PAUL GEIGER**
ART DIRECTOR: DENISE CRONIN
PUBLISHER: KNOPF/PANTHEON BOOKS FOR YOUNG READERS

# JURY

**RAY AMEIJIDE,** CHAIRMAN
Freelance illustrator.

**TOM DALY**
Freelance illustrator.

**ROBERT GIUSTI**
Freelance illustrator/designer,
servicing the record, advertising
and publishing businesses.

**GREG HILDEBRANDT**
Freelance illustrator specializing
in book illustration.

**CAROL LEITERMAN**
Vice President, Creative Director,
Edwin Bird Wilson Advertising,
Inc., Promotional Department.

**MICHAEL MENDELSOHN**
Creative Director, The Franklin
Library. Design Awards from the
Society, Art Directors Club, AIGA,
TDC and *Communication Arts.*

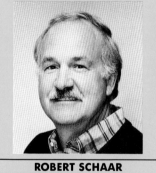

**ROBERT SCHAAR**
Painter/illustrator specializing in
figure and sports illustration. A
NASA artist he's participated
in Air Force Art Programs for
16 years.

**LYNN SWEAT**
Illustrator/painter.

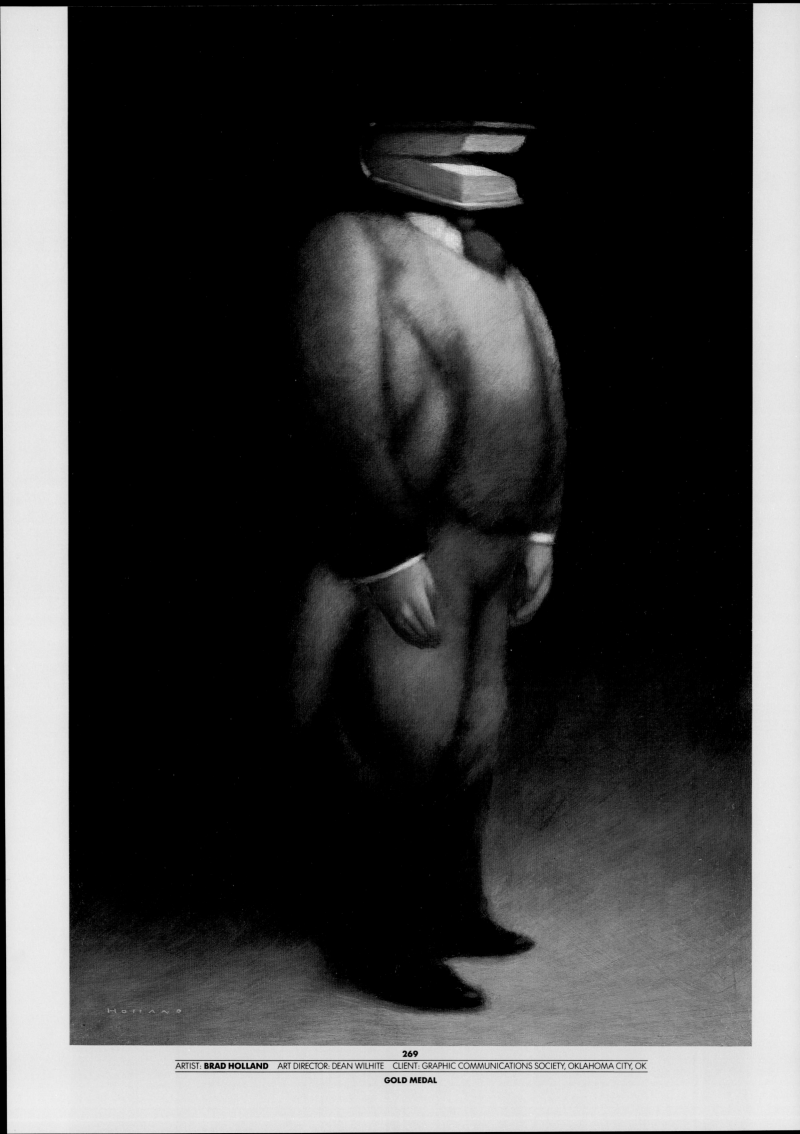

**269**
ARTIST: **BRAD HOLLAND**    ART DIRECTOR: DEAN WILHITE    CLIENT: GRAPHIC COMMUNICATIONS SOCIETY, OKLAHOMA CITY, OK

**GOLD MEDAL**

**270**

ARTIST: **MAX GINSBURG**

**GOLD MEDAL**

**271**

ARTIST: **ALEX MURAWSKI**    ART DIRECTOR: DAVID BARTELS    AGENCY: BARTELS & COMPANY    CLIENT: BRUCE BENDINGER

**GOLD MEDAL**

**272**
ARTIST: **IVAN POWELL**   ART DIRECTOR: DEVON HAPPERSET   CLIENT: SMITH KLINE

**SILVER MEDAL**

**273**

ARTIST: **BRALDT BRALDS**    ART DIRECTOR: FRANK C. LIONETTI    CLIENT: TREFOIL DEVELOPMENT COMPANY

**SILVER MEDAL**

274
ARTIST: **BOB CROFUT**

275
ARTIST: **MAX GINSBURG**

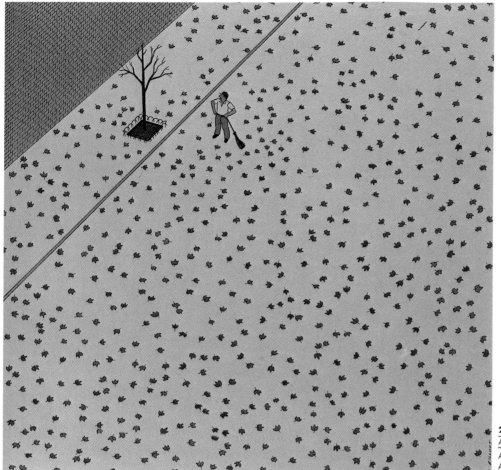

**276**
ARTIST: **GUY BILLOUT**
ART DIRECTOR: DAVID SAVINAR
AGENCY: EDWIN BIRD WILSON
CLIENT: BACCALA & SHOOP

**277**
ARTIST: **TOM CURRY**
ART DIRECTOR: GORDON MORTENSEN
PHIL RAYMOND
PUBLISHER: APPLE MAGAZINE

**278**
ARTIST: **PAUL CALLE**
ART DIRECTOR: ELLEN PEDERSEN
CLIENT: WESTERN HERITAGE SALE

**279**
ARTIST: **LUIGI CASTIGLIONI**
ART DIRECTOR: CAROLE GRAEBNER
CLIENT: MUTUAL BENEFIT LIFE

**280**
ARTIST: **MICHAEL G. COBB**
ART DIRECTOR: GEORGE OSAKI
CLIENT: MCA RECORDS

**281**

ARTIST: **ED PARKER**

ART DIRECTOR: DEBBIE LUCKE
AGENCY: JOHN PEARSON INC.
CLIENT: PUBLICK HOUSE

**282**

ARTIST: **GARRY COLBY**

ART DIRECTOR: BOB FORLENZA
AGENCY: CAMPBELL EWALD
CLIENT: K MART

283
ARTIST: **FANNY MELLET BERRY**
ART DIRECTOR: WALTER LEFMANN
CLIENT: TIME MAGAZINE

284
ARTIST: **DON WELLER**
ART DIRECTOR: WALLY RUNNELS
AGENCY: KRESSER & ROBBINS
CLIENT: STAR SOFTWARE

**285**
ARTIST: **LESLIE WU**   ART DIRECTOR: LESLIE WU   CLIENT: IPS MACDONALD COMPANY INC.

**286**
ARTIST: **C.F. PAYNE**

ART DIRECTOR: KENT L. EGGLESTON
AGENCY: BROYLES, ALLEBAUGH, DAVIS, INC.
CLIENT: MANVILLE CORPORATION

**287**
ARTIST: **MICHAEL SCHWAB**

ART DIRECTOR: JEFFREY WALKER
CLIENT: WILKES BASHFORD

**288**
ARTIST: **ROBERT HEINDEL**
ART DIRECTOR: MARTY GIURICCO
AGENCY: EDWIN BIRD WILSON
CLIENT: MANUFACTURERS HANOVER

**289**
ARTIST: **ROBERT GROSSMAN**
ART DIRECTOR: TONY LANE/NANCY DONALD
CLIENT: CBS RECORDS

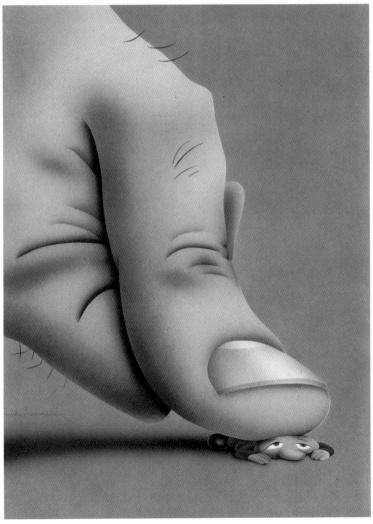

**290**
ARTIST: **BOB CONGE**

ART DIRECTOR: ROBERT MAHARRY
AGENCY: HUTCHINS Y&R
CLIENT: ROCHESTER CHAMBER OF COMMERCE

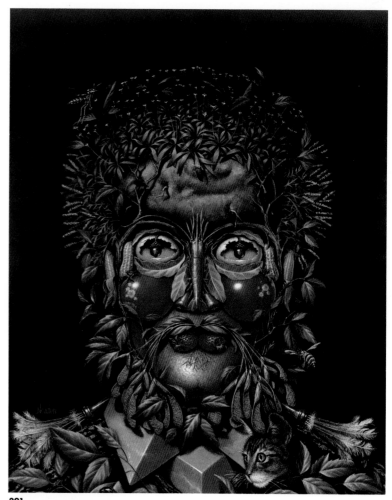

**291**
ARTIST: **RICHARD NEWTON**

ART DIRECTOR: JOHN HEDQUIST
AGENCY: TRECO ADVERTISING
CLIENT: PHARMACIA DIAGNOSTICS

292
ARTIST: **DENIS HAGEN**

ART DIRECTOR: DENIS HAGEN
AGENCY: BOZELL & JACOBS
CLIENT: ILLINOIS STATE LOTTERY

**293**
ARTIST: **LEO & DIANE DILLON**
ART DIRECTOR: MICHAEL GOODE
CLIENT: CAEDMON

**294**
ARTIST: **MARGARET CUSACK**
ART DIRECTOR: RUBIN PFEFFER
CLIENT: HARCOURT BRACE JOVANOVICH

**295**
ARTIST: **LYN BOYER-PENNINGTON**

ART DIRECTOR: LYN BOYER-PENNINGTON
CLIENT: ROOFTOP RECORDS

**296**
ARTIST: **ALEX GNIDZIEJKO**

ART DIRECTOR: KATHLEEN CREIGHTON/STEPHEN BODKIN
CLIENT: RSVP: THE DIRECTORY OF CREATIVE TALENT

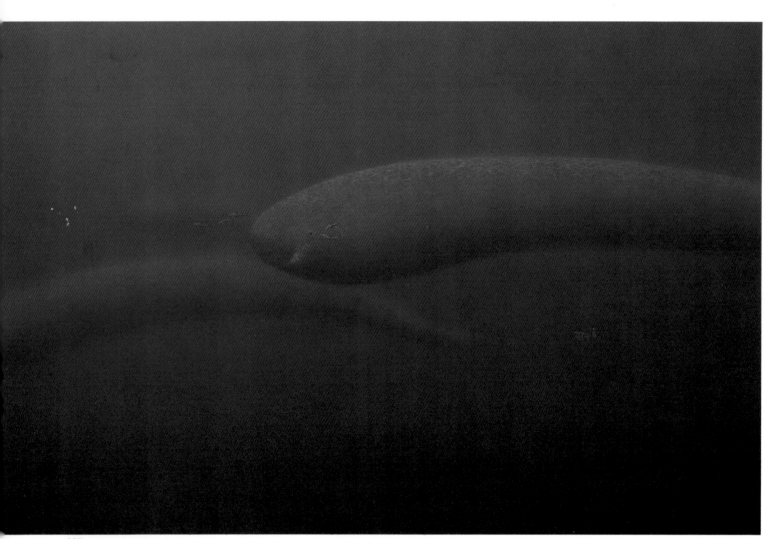

**297**
ARTIST: **JERRY LOFARO**

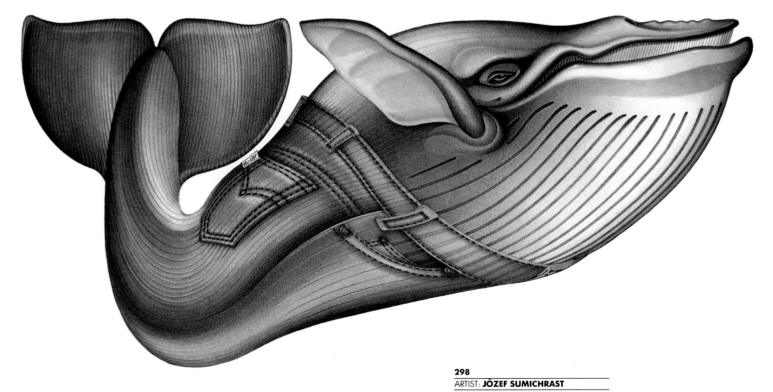

**298**
ARTIST: **JÒZEF SUMICHRAST**

ART DIRECTOR: GLEN DECICCO
AGENCY: FOOTE, CONE, BELDING, HONIG
CLIENT: LEVI'S

**299**
ARTIST: **DON WELLER**    ART DIRECTOR: JIM CROSS    CLIENT: SIMPSON PAPER COMPANY

**300**
ARTIST: **JERRY LOFARO**

**301**
ARTIST: **MARSHALL ARISMAN**

ART DIRECTOR: KEN PETRETTI
CLIENT: ABC

**302**
ARTIST: **FRED OTNES**
ART DIRECTOR: MARGRIT KAESER
CLIENT: REGENTS PUBLISHING COMPANY

**303**
ARTIST: **BRAD HOLLAND**
ART DIRECTOR: SHERRY POLLACK
AGENCY: McCAFFREY & McCALL
CLIENT: EXXON PBS

**304**
ARTIST: **ALEX MURAWSKI**

ART DIRECTOR: ROBERT QUALLY
AGENCY: QUALLY & COMPANY INC.
CLIENT: NABISCO BRANDS

**305**
ARTIST: **TOM NIKOSEY**

ART DIRECTOR: RICHARD LEBENSON/KATHLEEN CREIGHTON
CLIENT: RSVP: THE DIRECTORY OF CREATIVE TALENT

**306**
ARTIST: **RHONDA NASS**
ART DIRECTOR: JEFF LARSON
CLIENT: JEFF LARSON

**307**
ARTIST: **ROBERT RODRIGUEZ**
ART DIRECTOR: TOM CORCORAN
AGENCY: BUSCH CREATIVE
CLIENT: BUDWEISER BEER

308

ARTIST: **MELANIE MARDER PARKS**   ART DIRECTOR: KEITH SHERIDAN   CLIENT: RANDOM HOUSE

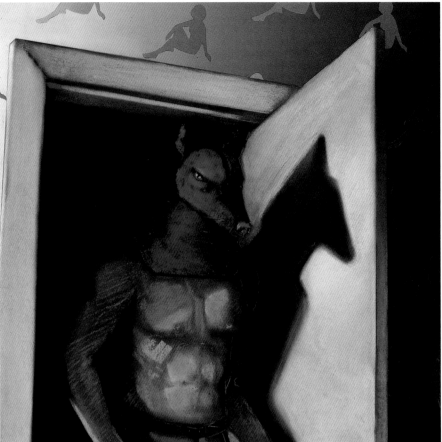

**309**
ARTIST: **SANDRA FILIPPUCCI**

**310**
ARTIST: **BIRNEY LETTICK**

ART DIRECTOR: JIM CLARKE
AGENCY: THE BLOOM AGENCY
CLIENT: MOOSEHEAD BEER

**311**
ARTIST: **TOM CURRY**

ART DIRECTOR: TOM CURRY
CLIENT: WALLACE ENGRAVING COMPANY

**312**
ARTIST: **RICHARD HESS**

ART DIRECTOR: KEN PETRETTI
CLIENT: ABC

**313**
ARTIST: **KAREN WATSON**
ART DIRECTOR: WENDY HILGERT
AGENCY: INGALLS
CLIENT: COPLEY PLACE

**314**
ARTIST: **ROBERT WEAVER**
ART DIRECTOR: SILAS RHODES
CLIENT: SCHOOL OF VISUAL ARTS

**315**
ARTIST: **DOUG ROSENTHAL**

ART DIRECTOR: CAREN MARTINEAU
AGENCY: ASH LeDONNE
CLIENT: RADIO CITY MUSIC HALL

**316**
ARTIST: **LINDA FENNIMORE**

ART DIRECTOR: DONN DAVENPORT
CLIENT: ARISTA RECORDS

**317**
ARTIST: **ROBERT J. KUESTER**

**318**
ARTIST: **PAUL DAVIS**

ART DIRECTOR: RICH MARTEL
AGENCY: B.B.D.&O. INC.
CLIENT: GENERAL ELECTRIC

**319**
ARTIST: **BERNIE KARLIN**

**320**
ARTIST: **C. PHILLIP WIKOFF**

**321**
ARTIST: **NICK CHARLES STAMAS**
ART DIRECTOR: NICK CHARLES STAMAS
CLIENT: ROSS LABORATORIES

**322**
ARTIST: **MURRAY TINKELMAN**

**323**
ARTIST: **JAVIER ROMERO**   ART DIRECTOR: JAVIER ATELA   AGENCY: J. WALTER THOMPSON   CLIENT: MONET JEWELERS

**324**
ARTIST: **BARBARA FOX**

**325**

ARTIST: **WILL WILSON**

ART DIRECTOR: JEFF WILSON
AGENCY: WILSON & PECK
CLIENT: ART LITHO COMPANY

**326**

ARTIST: **CAROL WALD**

ART DIRECTOR: RICHARD LAURENCE STEVENS
CLIENT: HOECHST-ROUSSEL PHARMACEUTICALS

**327**
ARTIST: **MILTON GLASER**
ART DIRECTOR: SHERRY POLLACK
AGENCY: McCAFFREY & McCALL
CLIENT: EXXON PBS

**328**
ARTIST: **ROGER HUYSSEN**
ART DIRECTOR: JOHN BERG
CLIENT: CBS RECORDS

**329**
ARTIST: **SEYMOUR CHWAST**

ART DIRECTOR: LILA STERNGLASS
AGENCY: RUMRILL-HOYT
CLIENT: NEW YORK CITY OPERA

**330**
ARTIST: **MARK CHICKINELLI**

ART DIRECTOR: PATTI O'NEILL/MARK CHICKINELLI
CLIENT: SOKAL HALL

**331**

ARTIST: **EUGENE MIHAESCO**

ART DIRECTOR: GERRY O'HARA
AGENCY: EPSTEIN, RABOY ADVERTISING
CLIENT: AFIA WORLDWIDE INSURANCE

**332**
ARTIST: **JOHN BERKEY**

ART DIRECTOR: WALTER KOLLIGS
AGENCY: COMPTON ADVERTISING
CLIENT: U.S. STEEL

**333**
ARTIST: **BERNIE KARLIN**

**334**
ARTIST: **JIM STARR**

335
ARTIST: **MURRAY TINKELMAN**

336
ARTIST: **REYNOLD RUFFINS**
ART DIRECTOR: JIM MALTESE
AGENCY: WUNDERMAN, RICOTTA & KLINE
CLIENT: C.I.T.

337
ARTIST: **ANN MANRY KENYON**
ART DIRECTOR: RAY ERNST
CLIENT: R.J. ERNST ENTERPRISES

338
ARTIST: **MARK GRAHAM**

**339**
ARTIST: **RAFAL OLBINSKI**
ART DIRECTOR: TERELLE KRAUS
CLIENT: THE NEW YORK TIMES

**340**
ARTIST: **LARRY WINBORG**
ART DIRECTOR: TERRENCE MEAGHER
CLIENT: TEXAS INSTRUMENTS, INC.

**341**
ARTIST: **MARSHALL ARISMAN**
ART DIRECTOR: ALLEN WEINBERG
CLIENT: CBS RECORDS

**342**
ARTIST: **GLENN HARRINGTON**
ART DIRECTOR: NANCY SLIVKA
AGENCY: L.M. & P. ADVERTISING
CLIENT: ALCON LABORATORIES

**343**
ARTIST: **FRED OTNES**
ART DIRECTOR: GORDON FISHER
CLIENT: NEENAH PAPER

**345**
ARTIST: **MICHAEL DAVID BROWN**

ART DIRECTOR: GINI BICKET
AGENCY: GARDNER ADVERTISING COMPANY
CLIENT: IC INDUSTRIES

**344**
ARTIST: **ALEX EBEL**

ART DIRECTOR: RON WOLIN
AGENCY: DANCER, FITZGERALD, SAMPLE
CLIENT: BRIDGESTONE TIRE COMPANY OF AMERICA

**346**
ARTIST: **RICK GRIMES**

ART DIRECTOR: PAT DeBLANC
CLIENT: MITSUBISHI AIRCRAFT

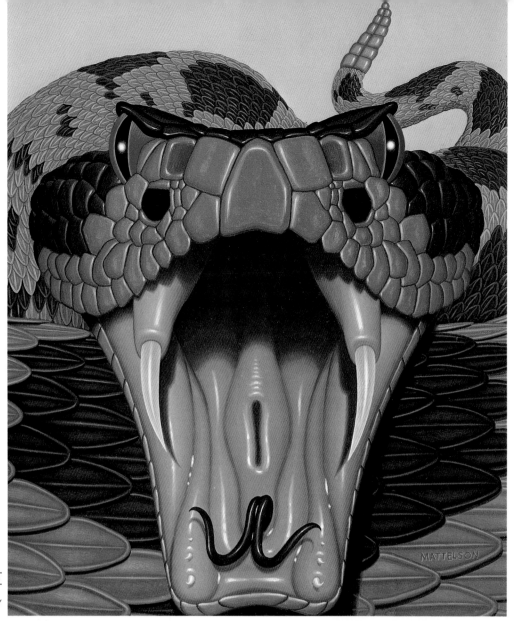

347
ARTIST: **MARVIN MATTELSON**

ART DIRECTOR: DAVID BARTELS
AGENCY: BARTELS & COMPANY
CLIENT: ANHEUSER-BUSCH

348
ARTIST: **JOHN P. TIERNEY**

**349**
ARTIST: **ALEX EBEL**
ART DIRECTOR: MARK KELLER
AGENCY: ACKERMAN & McQUEEN ADVERTISING INC.
CLIENT: NOCONA BOOT COMPANY

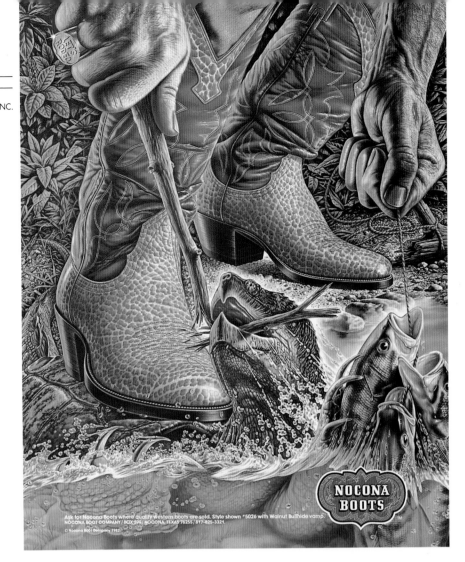

**350**
ARTIST: **ALEX MURAWSKI**
ART DIRECTOR: DAVID BARTELS
AGENCY: BARTELS & COMPANY
CLIENT: ANHEUSER-BUSCH

**351**
ARTIST: **BRAD HOLLAND**
ART DIRECTOR: JOHN BERG/ALLEN WEINBERG
CLIENT: CBS RECORDS

**352**
ARTIST: **LINDAH LAUDERBAUGH**
ART DIRECTOR: LINDAH LAUDERBAUGH
CLIENT: OUTSIDE RECORDS

**353**
ARTIST: **NORMAN WALKER**
ART DIRECTOR: BOB DEFRIN
CLIENT: ATLANTIC RECORDS

**354**
ARTIST: **SIMMS TABACK**

ART DIRECTOR: LESLIE SCHECT
CLIENT: AIG

**355**
ARTIST: **TOM NACHREINER**

ART DIRECTOR: TOM NACHREINER
CLIENT: ARTHUR WETZEL PRINTING

**356**
ARTIST: **ROBERT G. STEELE**
ART DIRECTOR: G. GROOT
CLIENT: CROW-SPIEKER

**357**
ARTIST: **GARY MEYER**
ART DIRECTOR: BARRY DEUTSCH
CLIENT: VISICORP

M. LANGENECKERT ©1981

**358**
ARTIST: **MARK LANGENECKERT**
ART DIRECTOR: THERESE FLEETWOOD
CLIENT: BRANDWOOD PRODUCTIONS

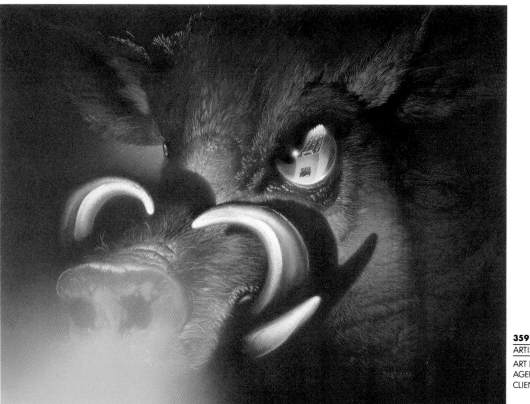

**359**
ARTIST: **ROBERT RODRIGUEZ**
ART DIRECTOR: JOHN SAFRIT/DOUG HILL
AGENCY: LEWIS, GILMAN & KYNETT, INC.
CLIENT: EXIDE BATTERIES

**360**
ARTIST: **BRUCE WALDMAN**

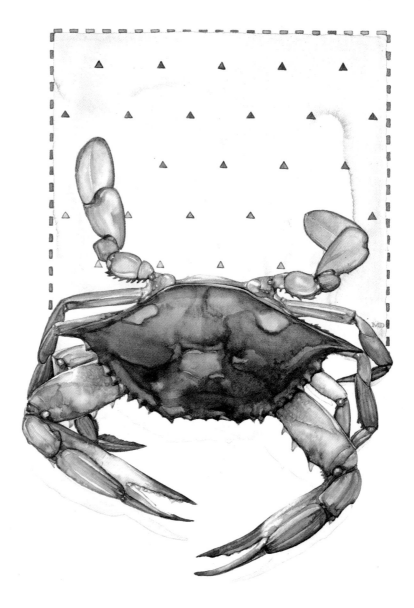

**361**
ARTIST: **MICHAEL DEAN**

ART DIRECTOR: HUGH McDONNOLD
AGENCY: MDR, INC.
CLIENT: SHELL CHEMICAL COMPANY

**362**
ARTIST: **JILL KARLA SCHWARZ**

ART DIRECTOR: KEITH GOLD
AGENCY: PRICE/McNABB
CLIENT: COVINGTON SQUARE

**363**
ARTIST: **TOMIE dePAOLA**

ART DIRECTOR: TOMIE dePAOLA
CLIENT: THE VANESSA-ANN COLLECTION

364
ARTIST: **JUDY PEDERSEN**

**369**
ARTIST: **DENNIS LUZAK**
ART DIRECTOR: DENNIS LUZAK
CLIENT: PATELLA AGENCY

**370**
ARTIST: **GREG RUDD**
ART DIRECTOR: JERRY LEOPOLD
AGENCY: POPPE TYSON
CLIENT: POLYTECNIC

**371**
ARTIST: **NORMAN WALKER**
ART DIRECTOR: SANDRA RUCH
CLIENT: MOBIL OIL CORPORATION

**372**
ARTIST: **MARSHALL ARISMAN**
ART DIRECTOR: KEN PETRETTI
CLIENT: ABC

**373**
ARTIST: **GARY KELLEY**
ART DIRECTOR: DICK BLAZEK
CLIENT: IOWA SHAKESPEARE FESTIVAL

ARTIST: **ALAN HASSINGER**

**375**
ARTIST: **MICHAEL GARLAND**

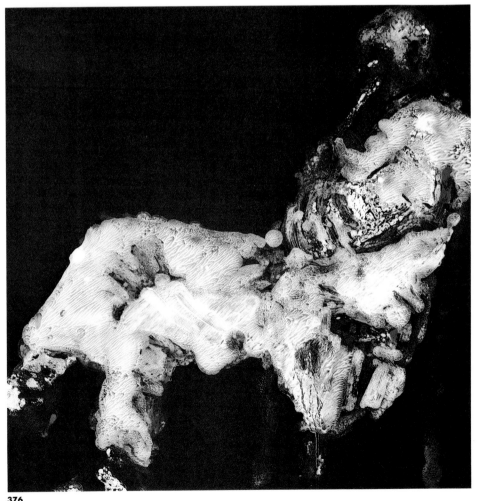

**376**
ARTIST: **DAVID LIMRITE**

ART DIRECTOR: DAVID LIMRITE
CLIENT: MONTEREY JAZZ FESTIVAL

**377**
ARTIST: **LON BUSCH**

ART DIRECTOR: ART MAAS
CLIENT: ANHEUSER-BUSCH

**378**
ARTIST: **M. JOHN ENGLISH**    ART DIRECTOR: SUSAN BAKER    CLIENT: HUFFY CORPORATION

**379**
ARTIST: **ROBERT HEINDEL**    ART DIRECTOR: ROBERT HEINDEL    CLIENT: SAN FRANCISCO BALLET

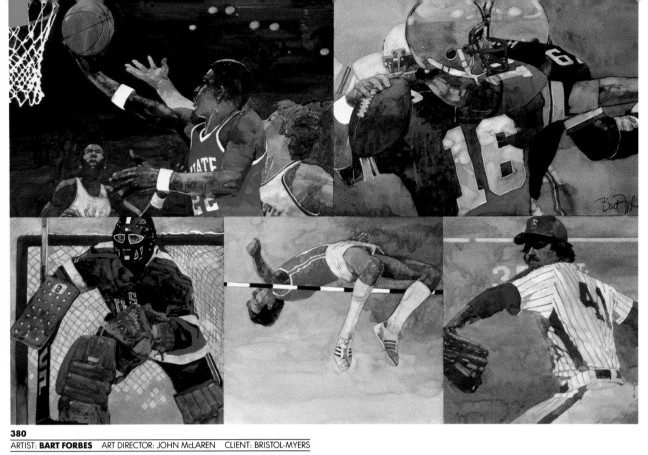

**380**
ARTIST: **BART FORBES**    ART DIRECTOR: JOHN McLAREN    CLIENT: BRISTOL-MYERS

**381**
ARTIST: **DON WELLER**
ART DIRECTOR: JON ANDERSON/MIKIO OSAKI
CLIENT: TDCTJHTBIPC

**382**

ARTIST: **NOXX**

ART DIRECTOR: BILLY GIBBONS
CLIENT: LONE WOLF PRODUCTIONS

**383**
ARTIST: **EDWARD SOREL**
ART DIRECTOR: JIM JOHNSTON
AGENCY: JIM JOHNSTON ADVERTISING
CLIENT: DREXEL BURNHAM LAMBERT

**384**
ARTIST: **CHARLES SANTORE**
ART DIRECTOR: JEAN YAMADA
AGENCY: N.W. AYER INTERNATIONAL
CLIENT: TV GUIDE

385
ARTIST: **NICHOLAS GAETANO**    ART DIRECTOR: CLARICE BONZER    AGENCY: TRACY-LOCKE/B.B.D.&O.    CLIENT: FRONTIER AIRLINES

386
ARTIST: **JOE ISOM**    ART DIRECTOR: JOE VANHOSEN    AGENCY: BOZELL & JACOBS    CLIENT: MUTUAL OF OMAHA

387

ARTIST: **TERESA FASOLINO**

ART DIRECTOR: NORMAN UNG
CLIENT: ELEKTRA/ASYLUM/NONESUCH RECORDS

388

ARTIST: **JACKIE GEYER**

ART DIRECTOR: JOHN BORMANN
AGENCY: YOUNG & RUBICAM
CLIENT: TIME INCORPORATED

**389**
ARTIST: **JAMES McMULLAN**
ART DIRECTOR: JAMES McMULLAN
CLIENT: GIRAFFICS

**390**
ARTIST: **BRIAN ZICK/WAYNE McLAUGHLIN**
ART DIRECTOR: ANNE OCCI/BRETT SHEVACK
AGENCY: LAURENCE, CHARLES & FREE
CLIENT: ADIDAS, USA

**391**

ARTIST: **WILLIAM LOW**

ART DIRECTOR: EMIL MICHA/ANDREW KNER
CLIENT: THE NEW YORK TIMES

**392**

ARTIST: **ROBERT M. CUNNINGHAM**

ART DIRECTOR: CLAUDIA MENGEL
CLIENT: MANUFACTURERS HANOVER TRUST

**393**

ARTIST: **LON BUSCH**

ART DIRECTOR: DAVID BARTELS
AGENCY: BARTELS & COMPANY
CLIENT: ANHEUSER-BUSCH

**394**

ARTIST: **LON BUSCH**

ART DIRECTOR: EDWARD VERNON
AGENCY: STOLZ ADVERTISING
CLIENT: McDONALD'S

**395**

ARTIST: **ED LINDLOF**

ART DIRECTOR: PEGGY McDANIEL
AGENCY: THE HINCKLEY GROUP
CLIENT: GARY L. CUTSINGER COMPANY

**396**

ARTIST: **ED LINDLOF**

ART DIRECTOR: CODY NEWMAN
AGENCY: ROSENBERG & COMPANY
CLIENT: SPRING CREEK INVESTMENTS

**397**
ARTIST: **NICHOLAS GAETANO**    ART DIRECTOR: CLARICE BONZER    AGENCY: TRACY-LOCKE/B.B.D.&O.    CLIENT: FRONTIER AIRLINES

**399**
ARTIST: **WILLIAM HILLENBRAND**
ART DIRECTOR: BARRON KRODY
CLIENT: CINCINNATI REGATTA 83

**398**
ARTIST: **JOHN SCHRECK**
ART DIRECTOR: BOB WILCOX
CLIENT: JOHN HANCOCK

**400**
ARTIST: **CATHY BARANCIK**
ART DIRECTOR: DIANA NILES
CLIENT: ULTIMA II/REVLON

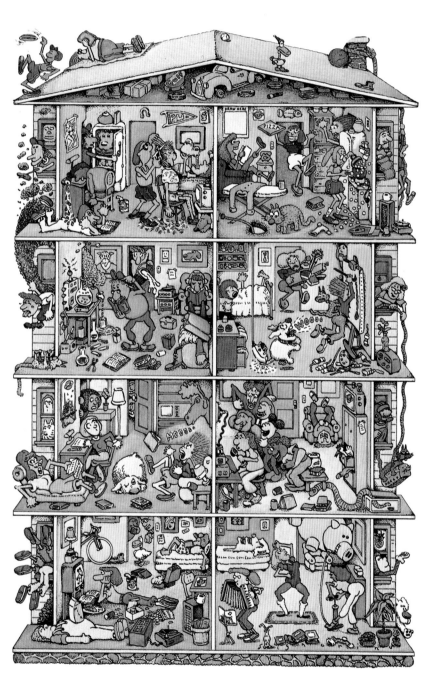

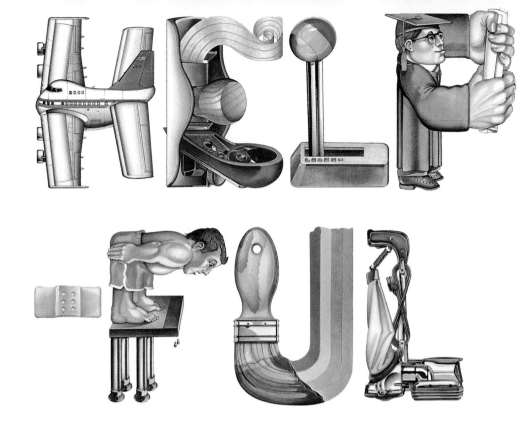

**403**

ARTIST: **JÓZEF SUMICHRAST**

ART DIRECTOR: JIM ROOT
AGENCY: NEEDHAM, HARPER & STEERS
CLIENT: HOUSEHOLD FINANCE

**404**

ARTIST: **BERNIE FUCHS**

ART DIRECTOR: PHIL GIPS
CLIENT: MOBIL OIL CORPORATION

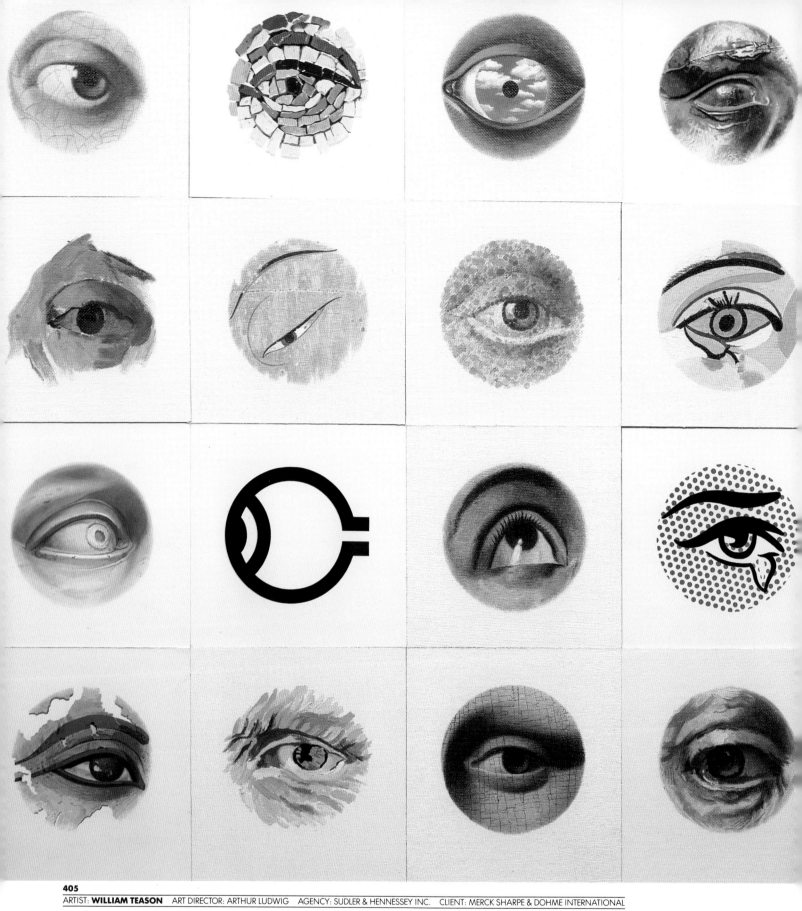

**405**
ARTIST: **WILLIAM TEASON**   ART DIRECTOR: ARTHUR LUDWIG   AGENCY: SUDLER & HENNESSEY INC.   CLIENT: MERCK SHARPE & DOHME INTERNATIONAL

**406**
ARTIST: **BERNIE KARLIN**

**407**
ARTIST: **MICKEY PARASKEVAS**

ART DIRECTOR: HARRY RIGBY
AGENCY: QUIST VISUALS
CLIENT: TERRY ALLEN KRAMER

**408**
ARTIST: **BOB CONGE**

ART DIRECTOR: BOB CONGE
CLIENT: CORN HILL NEIGHBORS ASSOCIATION

**409**

ARTIST: **ALAN HASHIMOTO**

ART DIRECTOR: GENE SULEK/STEVEN FORD
CLIENT: TEXAS INSTRUMENTS INC.

**410**

ARTIST: **JOHN FINDLEY**

ART DIRECTOR: SY GITELSON
AGENCY: GITEL, INC.
CLIENT: KENNESAW LIFE

© 1982 John Findley

**411**
ARTIST: **JOE HEINER**
ART DIRECTOR: ANNE OCCI/BRETT SHEVACK
AGENCY: LAURENCE, CHARLES & FREE
CLIENT: ADIDAS, USA

**412**
ARTIST: **ROBERT GOLDSTROM**
ART DIRECTOR: EMIL MICHA/ANDREW KNER
CLIENT: THE NEW YORK TIMES

**413**

ARTIST: **KEN GOLDAMMER**

ART DIRECTOR: LYN MORNINGSTAR
AGENCY: R.M. FELDMAN
CLIENT: MICROLAB INC.

**414**

ARTIST: **DAVID GROVE**

ART DIRECTOR: ROY ALEXANDER
CLIENT: WALT DISNEY PRODUCTIONS

**415**
ARTIST: **MARK CHICKINELLI**
ART DIRECTOR: MARK CHICKINELLI/MICHAEL KLUG
CLIENT: OPERA/OMAHA

**416**
ARTIST: **RICHARD MANTEL**
ART DIRECTOR: ALEX GOTFRYD
CLIENT: DOUBLEDAY

**417**

ARTIST: **GERRY GERSTEN**

ART DIRECTOR: YURIKO GAMO
AGENCY: LORD, GELLER, FEDERICO, EINSTEIN
CLIENT: QUALITY PAPER BACK

**418**

ARTIST: **GERRY GERSTEN**

ART DIRECTOR: D.J. STOUT
AGENCY: ROBERT A. WILSON
CLIENT: HORCHOW COLLECTION

**419**

ARTIST: **GERRY GERSTEN**

ART DIRECTOR: D.J. STOUT
AGENCY: ROBERT A. WILSON
CLIENT: HORCHOW COLLECTION

**420**
ARTIST: **MARVIN MATTELSON**
ART DIRECTOR: ANN PROCHAZKA
AGENCY: VAN SANT DUGDALE
CLIENT: WESTINGHOUSE DEFENSE

**421**
ARTIST: **ALEX MURAWSKI**
ART DIRECTOR: DAVID BARTELS
AGENCY: BARTELS & COMPANY
CLIENT: MASTER TYPOGRAPHERS

**422**

ARTIST: **TOM HALLMAN**

ART DIRECTOR: GLENN BROWN
AGENCY: BROWN & KOSA, INC.
CLIENT: DIAGNOSTICS DESIGN

**423**

ARTIST: **ROBERT GOLDSTROM**

ART DIRECTOR: ALLEN WEINBERG
CLIENT: CBS RECORDS

**425**
ARTIST: **MARK POLLARD**    ART DIRECTOR: MARIAN LINDHOLTZ    AGENCY: D'ARCY McMANUS MANIUS    CLIENT: HUDSON STREET STUDIOS

**426**
ARTIST: **TOM CURRY**
ART DIRECTOR: CODY NEWMAN
AGENCY: ROSENBERG & COMPANY
CLIENT: WINDSONG CUSTOM HOMES

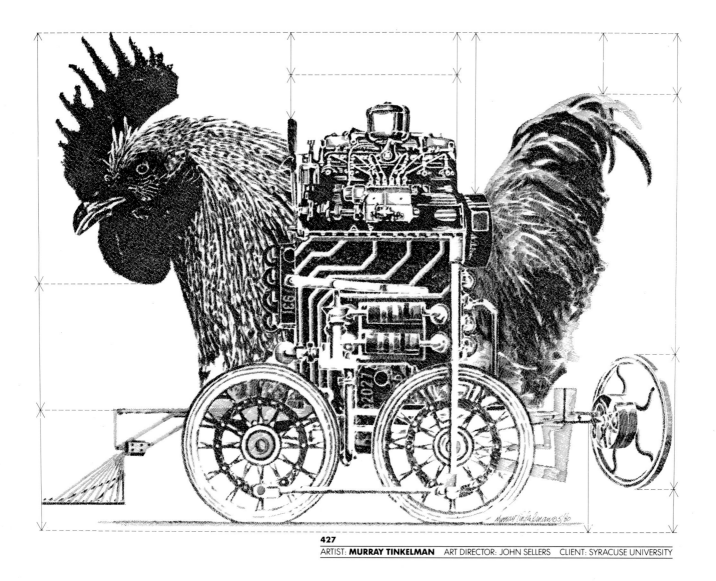

**427**
ARTIST: **MURRAY TINKELMAN**    ART DIRECTOR: JOHN SELLERS    CLIENT: SYRACUSE UNIVERSITY

ARTIST: **VIVIENNE FLESHER**    ART DIRECTOR: LINDA EVANS    CLIENT: NEW PARENT SERIES

**429**
ARTIST: **BARBARA MASLEN**

ART DIRECTOR: BETH GEROWITZ
CLIENT: COLLINS & AIKMAN

**430**
ARTIST: **LUIS R. CUEVAS**

ART DIRECTOR: ROBERT TALARCZYK
AGENCY: C & G AGENCY
CLIENT: CIBA-GEIGY PHARMACEUTICALS

**431**

ARTIST: **TERESA FASOLINO**

ART DIRECTOR: RANDALL HENSLEY
AGENCY: MUIR CORNELIUS MOORE
CLIENT: UNITED TELECOM COMPUTER GROUP

**432**

ARTIST: **RHONDA NASS**

CLIENT: ILLUSTRATORS WORKSHOP

**433**
ARTIST: **LYNN SWEAT**

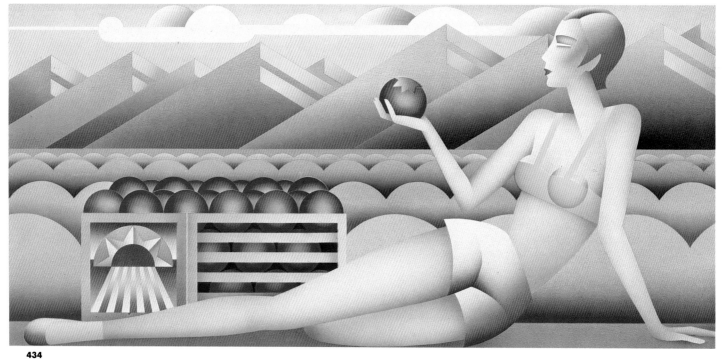

**434**
ARTIST: **NICHOLAS GAETANO**

ART DIRECTOR: CLARICE BONZER
AGENCY: TRACY-LOCKE/B.B.D.&O.
CLIENT: FRONTIER AIRLINES

**435**
ARTIST: **GEORGE STAVRINOS**
CLIENT: BERGDORF GOODMAN

**436**
ARTIST: **GEORGE STAVRINOS**
CLIENT: BERGDORF GOODMAN

**437**
ARTIST: **BILL NELSON**

ART DIRECTOR: RANDY SHERMAN
CLIENT: PALMER PAPER COMPANY

**438**
ARTIST: **ARTHUR LIDOV**

ART DIRECTOR: BURTON POLLACK
AGENCY: BARNUM COMMUNICATIONS, INC.
CLIENT: BOEHRINGER INGELHEIM

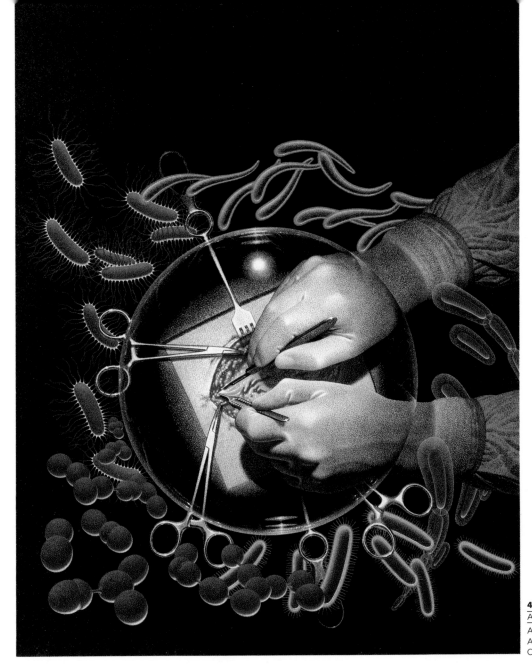

**439**
ARTIST: **EDWARD GAZSI**

ART DIRECTOR: ROGER MUSICH
AGENCY: KLEMTNER ADVERTISING, INC.
CLIENT: SCHERING INTERNATIONAL

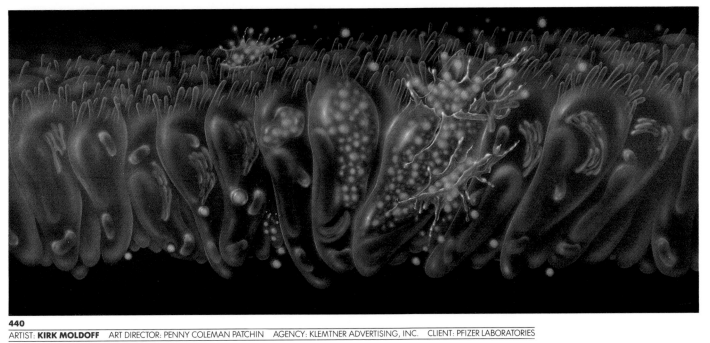

**440**
ARTIST: **KIRK MOLDOFF**    ART DIRECTOR: PENNY COLEMAN PATCHIN    AGENCY: KLEMTNER ADVERTISING, INC.    CLIENT: PFIZER LABORATORIES

**441**
ARTIST: **DOUG JOHNSON**
ART DIRECTOR: KEITH BRIGHT
CLIENT: HOLLAND AMERICA LINE

**442**
ARTIST: **MICHAEL SCHWAB**
ART DIRECTOR: CAROLYN BRENNAN
JIM GEORGEDES
CLIENT: WILKES BASHFORD

**443**
ARTIST: **ALBERT LORENZ**
ART DIRECTOR: TOSHIAKI IDE
AGENCY: WELLS RICH GREENE INC.
CLIENT: PAN AM

444
ARTIST: **WENDY L. BURDEN**     ART DIRECTOR: EVA PIETRZAK     CLIENT: CONRAN'S

# JURY

**JIM SHARPE,** CHAIRMAN
Freelance illustrator.

**HAL ASHMEAD**
Freelance illustrator, participated in Air Force Art Programs. Exhibited at Grand Central Art Gallery.

**GUY BILLOUT**
Freelance illustrator.

**LOU BROOKS**
Designer/illustrator. Jury Chairman, New Illustration Show at Society of Illustrators. Awards from the Society, AIGA, American Illustration and *Graphic Design USA.*

**ELLEN GRIESEDIECK**
Freelance illustrator and photographer.

**JAMES McMULLAN**
Freelance illustrator, author, past Vice President of AIGA, instructor of Masters Degree Program at SVA. One-man shows at Society of Illustrators and AIGA.

**CARL MOLNO**
Illustrator and watercolor teacher. Exhibitions at American Watercolor Society, National Academy of Design and Parrish Art Museum.

**445**

ARTIST: **REGAN DUNNICK**    ART DIRECTOR: STEVEN SESSIONS    AGENCY: STEVEN SESSIONS DESIGN    CLIENT: FIDELITY PRINTING

**SILVER MEDAL**

**446**

ARTIST: **MILTON GLASER**    ART DIRECTOR: MILTON GLASER    CLIENT: THE NEW YORK ZOOLOGICAL SOCIETY

**SILVER MEDAL**

**447**

ARTIST: **GERALD J. MONLEY, JR.**

**SILVER MEDAL**

**448**

ARTIST: **BRALDT BRALDS**     ART DIRECTOR: SHINICHIRO TORA/YASUHARU NAKAHARA     AGENCY: DNP AMERICA INC.     CLIENT: HOTEL BARMEN'S ASSOCIATION, JAPAN

**HAMILTON KING AWARD**

**SILVER MEDAL**

**449**
ARTIST: **SUSAN STILLMAN**

**450**
ARTIST: **MAX GINSBURG**

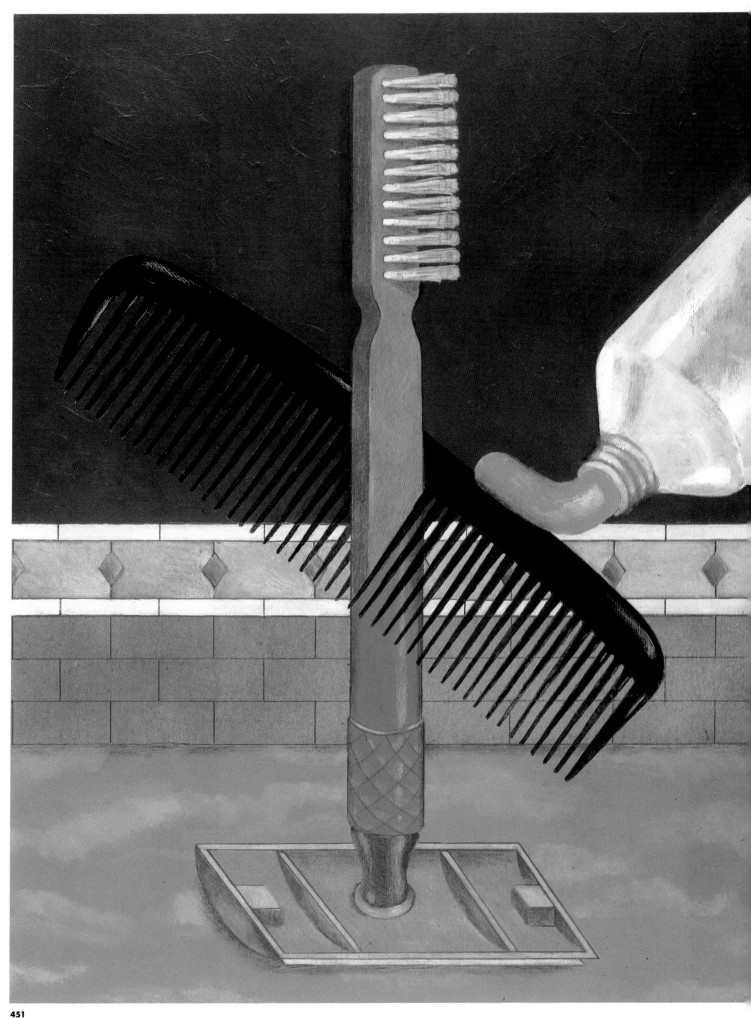

ARTIST: **SEYMOUR CHWAST**    ART DIRECTOR: JIM CROSS    CLIENT: SIMPSON PAPER COMPANY

**452**
ARTIST: **KAZUHIKO SANO**
ART DIRECTOR: KAZUHIKO SANO
CLIENT: THE SOURCE

453
ARTIST: **NANCY NILES**
ART DIRECTOR: NANCY NILES
CLIENT: HELLMAN ASSOCIATES

454
ARTIST: **WENDE L. CAPORALE**

**455**
ARTIST: **GARY KAEMMER**
ART DIRECTOR: GARY KAEMMER
CLIENT: SCOTTSWOOD PUBLICATIONS

**456**
ARTIST: **DAVID GROVE**
ART DIRECTOR: DAVID GROVE
CLIENT: SAN FRANCISCO BALLET

**457**
ARTIST: **JAMES McMULLAN**    ART DIRECTOR: SILAS RHODES    CLIENT: SCHOOL OF VISUAL ARTS

**458**
ARTIST: **RICHARD SPARKS**
ART DIRECTOR: RICH CARTER
CLIENT: MBI INC.

**459**
ARTIST: **NORMAN McDONALD**     ART DIRECTOR: PAUL HOYE/BRIAN SMITH     CLIENT: ARAMCO CORPORATION

**460**
ARTIST: **NORMAN McDONALD**     ART DIRECTOR: PAUL HOYE/BRIAN SMITH     CLIENT: ARAMCO CORPORATION

461
ARTIST: **DALE SIZER**
ART DIRECTOR: ROBERT M. FITCH
CLIENT: PAPER MOON GRAPHICS

462
ARTIST: **MICHAEL SCHWAB**    ART DIRECTOR: KEN WEBSTER    CLIENT: SHAKLEE CORPORATION

**463**
ARTIST: **PAUL MELIA**

ART DIRECTOR: GENE VANARD
CLIENT: THE GENERAL TIRE & RUBBER COMPANY

**464**
ARTIST: **RAFAL OLBINSKI**

ART DIRECTOR: RAFAL OLBINSKI
CLIENT: PAPERMANIA INTERNATIONAL

**465**
ARTIST: **JEFF LARAMORE**

ART DIRECTOR: JEFF LARAMORE
AGENCY: YOUNG & LARAMORE
CLIENT: PEARSON GROUP, INC.

**466**
ARTIST: **FRANCIS LIVINGSTON**

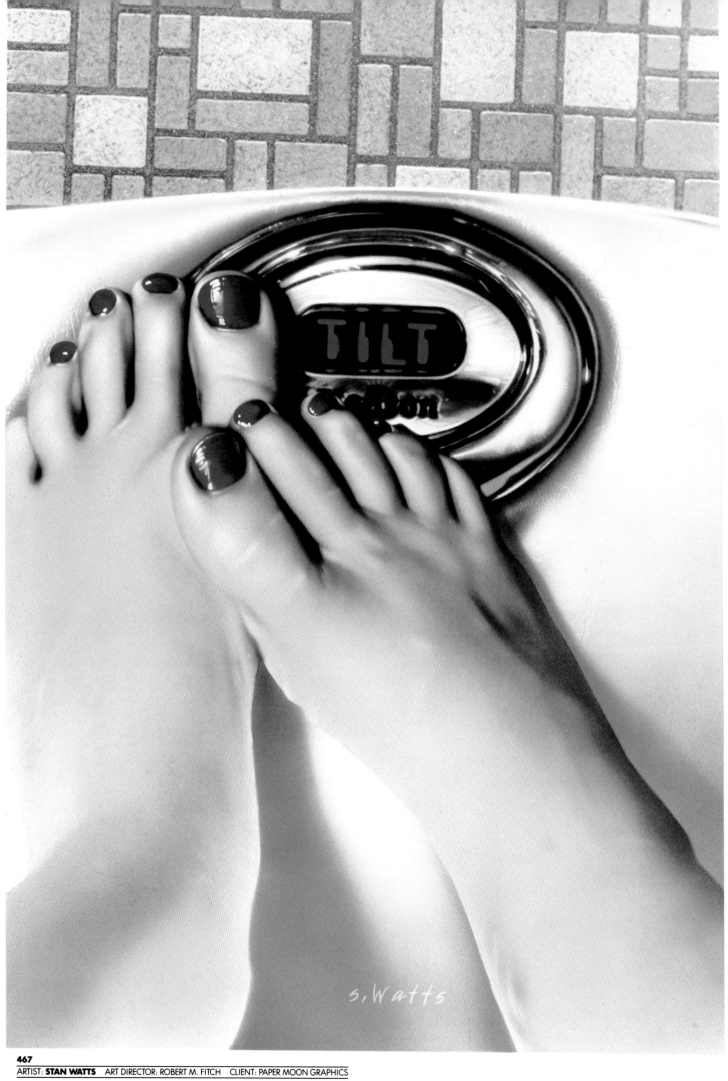

**467**
ARTIST: **STAN WATTS**    ART DIRECTOR: ROBERT M. FITCH    CLIENT: PAPER MOON GRAPHICS

**468**
ARTIST: **BOB SAINT JOHN**
CLIENT: ILLUSTRATORS WORKSHOP

**469**
ARTIST: **ALAN E. COBER**
ART DIRECTOR: SHINICHIRO TORA/YASUHARU NAKAHARA
AGENCY: DNP AMERICA INC.
CLIENT: HOTEL BARMEN'S ASSOCIATION, JAPAN

**470**
ARTIST: **ROBERT GIUSTI**    ART DIRECTOR: BENNETT ROBINSON/NAOMI BURSTEIN    CLIENT: ELI LILLY & COMPANY

**471**
ARTIST: **DEAN MITCHELL**

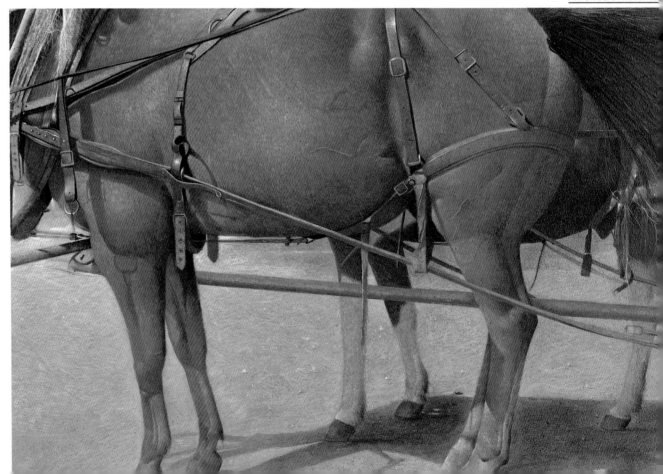

**472**

ARTIST: **ROBERT GIUSTI**

ART DIRECTOR: CRAIG BERNHARDT/JANET FUDYMA
CLIENT: W. R. GRACE & COMPANY

**473**

ARTIST: **JERRY PAVEY**

ART DIRECTOR: JERRY PAVEY
CLIENT: THE FEDERAL FARM CREDIT
BANKS FUNDING CORPORATION

**474**
ARTIST: **ROGER BERGENDORFF**
ART DIRECTOR: ROBERT M. FITCH
CLIENT: PAPER MOON GRAPHICS

**475**
ARTIST: **STEVE BARBARIA**

ART DIRECTOR: STEVE BARBARIA
CLIENT: CALIFORNIA PARKS & RECREATION DEPARTMENT

**476**
ARTIST: **PETE BIXLER**

ART DIRECTOR: PETE BIXLER/KATHERINE JOHNGEORGE
CLIENT: J. MOORE GALLERY

**477**
ARTIST: **ART CURTIS**

**478**
ARTIST: **ART CURTIS**

**479**
ARTIST: **MARK McMAHON**    ART DIRECTOR: LINDA VANDER WEELE    CLIENT: CHICAGO BOARD OF TRADE

**480**
ARTIST: **RENÉE FAURE**    ART DIRECTOR: MELANIE HART    CLIENT: VILLEROY & BOCH

**481**
ARTIST: **GARY KELLEY**    ART DIRECTOR: JOHN HALL    CLIENT: NORTHWEST IOWA SHOPPER

**482**
ARTIST: **KAREN JEAN PAYNE**

**483**
ARTIST: **TERRY WIDENER**

**486**

ARTIST: **MARGUERITA BORNSTEIN**

ART DIRECTOR: BOB PAGANUCCI/MARGARET WHITCHURCH
AGENCY: SALPETER PAGANUCCI INC.
CLIENT: GEIGY PHARMACEUTICALS

**488**

ARTIST: **SHELLEY DANIELS**

**487**

ARTIST: **SUE ELLEN BROWN**

ART DIRECTOR: DAVID BEITTEL
CLIENT: HALLMARK CARDS, INC.

**489**
ARTIST: **DARRYL ZUDECK**

**490**
ARTIST: **BILL CHARMATZ**

ART DIRECTOR: ELTON S. ROBINSON
CLIENT: EXXON CORPORATION

**491**
ARTIST: **DOUGLAS SMITH**

ART DIRECTOR: BOB MANLEY
CLIENT: ALTMAN & MANLEY

**492**
ARTIST: **BARRETT V. ROOT**

ART DIRECTOR: BOB EICHINGER/HOWARD RONDER
CLIENT: ST. REGIS

**495**
ARTIST: **BARRETT V. ROOT**

**496**
ARTIST: **STEVEN ASSEL**

**497**
ARTIST: **CHRIS VAN ALLSBURG**
ART DIRECTOR: CHRIS VAN ALLSBURG
CLIENT: AMERICAN LIBRARY ASSOCIATION

**498**
ARTIST: **MICHAEL GARLAND**
ART DIRECTOR: BRAD PALACE/HAROLD SITTERLY

**500**
ARTIST: **THOMAS M. SZUMOWSKI**

**501**
ARTIST: **BRALDT BRALDS**

ART DIRECTOR: DAVID BARTELS
AGENCY: BARTELS & COMPANY
CLIENT: UNIVERSITY OF CINCINNATI
FOOTBALL POSTER

**499**
ARTIST: **NICHOLAS GAETANO**

CLIENT: GEO

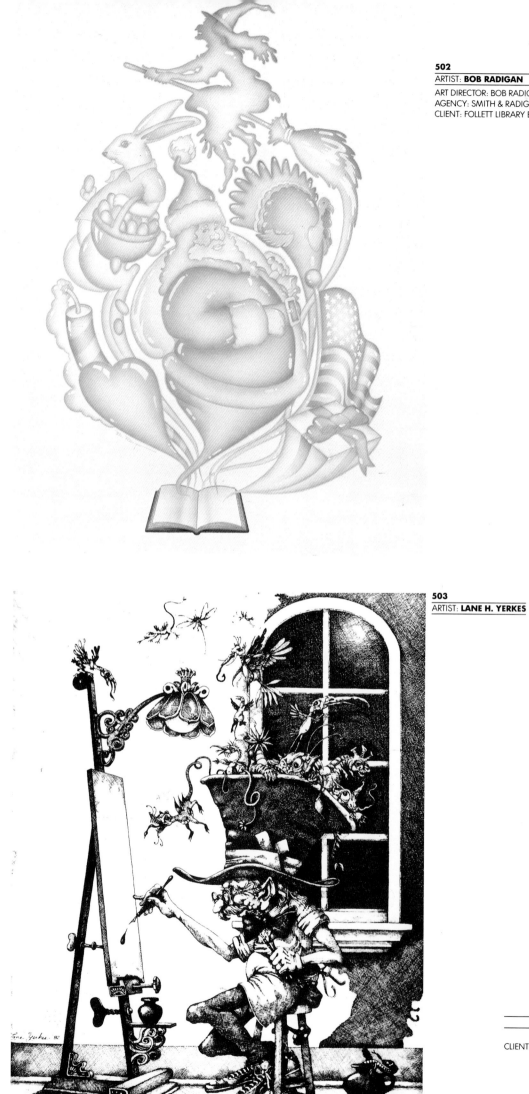

**502**
ARTIST: **BOB RADIGAN**

ART DIRECTOR: BOB RADIGAN
AGENCY: SMITH & RADIGAN ADVERTISING INC.
CLIENT: FOLLETT LIBRARY BOOK COMPANY

**503**
ARTIST: **LANE H. YERKES**

**504**
ARTIST: **MILTON GLASER**
ART DIRECTOR: MILTON GLASER
CLIENT: NEW YORK STATE DEPARTMENT OF COMMERCE

STEVEN SONDHEIM'S

THE DEMON BARBER
OF FLEET STREET

ARTIST: **BILL NELSON**    ART DIRECTOR: BILL NELSON    CLIENT: BARKSDALE THEATRE

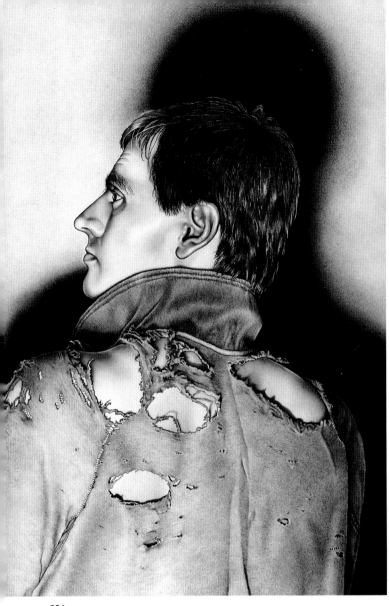

**506**
ARTIST: **NANCY LAWTON**

ART DIRECTOR: NANCY LAWTON

**507**
ARTIST: **JOANN DALEY**

ART DIRECTOR: ROBERT M. FITCH
CLIENT: PAPER MOON GRAPHICS

**508**
ARTIST: **WENDELIN EVE**

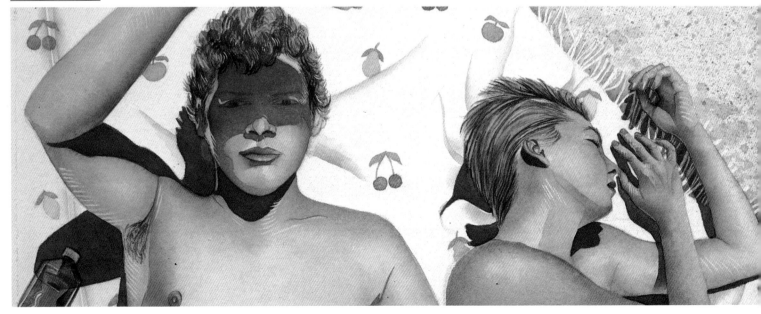

**509**
ARTIST: **WILLIAM BUERGE**　ART DIRECTOR: DIANA MARSHALL　CLIENT: LONG BEACH SAVINGS

510
ARTIST: **SUDI McCOLLUM**

ART DIRECTOR: SUDI McCOLLUM
CLIENT: McCOLLUM & PITCHER

511
ARTIST: **ARGUS CHILDERS**

ART DIRECTOR: DAVID BEITTEL/DON DUBOWSKI
CLIENT: HALLMARK CARDS, INC.

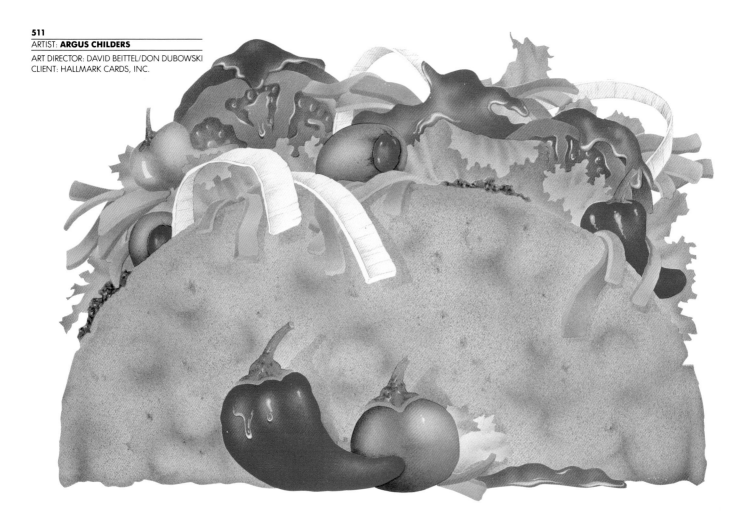

**512**
ARTIST: **WALTER FRANK BOMAR**

**513**
ARTIST: **MARTI BETZ**

ART DIRECTOR: MARTI BETZ
CLIENT: TOURISM COUNCIL OF ANNAPOLIS
& ANNE ARUNDEL COUNTY

**514**
ARTIST: **DAVID JEMERSON YOUNG**
ART DIRECTOR: DAVID JEMERSON YOUNG
AGENCY: YOUNG & LARAMORE
CLIENT: WIAN

515
ARTIST: **JOHN SPOSATO**
ART DIRECTOR: JOHN SPOSATO
CLIENT: F.P. COLOR SEPARATIONS

516
ARTIST: **DOUG JOHNSON**
ART DIRECTOR: DOUG JOHNSON/ANNE LEIGH
CLIENT: LA JOLLA PLAYHOUSE

Art Direction: David Bartels • Design & Typography: Strandell Baker • **Illustration: Alex Murawski** • Separations: Williams Litho • Printing: Sayers Communications Group

**517**
ARTIST: **ALEX MURAWSKI**

ART DIRECTOR: DAVID BARTELS
AGENCY: BARTELS & COMPANY
CLIENT: BRUCE BENDINGER

**518**
ARTIST: **MARGARET KASAHARA**

CLIENT: SIMPSON PAPER COMPANY

519
ARTIST: **CHRIS SPOLLEN**
ART DIRECTOR: ALICE DEGANHARDT
CLIENT: CREATIVE LIVING MAGAZINE

520
ARTIST: **MARVIN MATTELSON**
ART DIRECTOR: MARVIN MATTELSON
CLIENT: SOCIETY OF ILLUSTRATORS

**522**
ARTIST: **M.E. GATES**

ART DIRECTOR: M.E. GATES
CLIENT: NEW YORK TELEPHONE/
          NEW YORK SHAKESPEARE FESTIVAL

**523**
ARTIST: **ANN MEISEL**

**521**
ARTIST: **BERNARD GRANGER**

**524**
ARTIST: **BARBARA NESSIM**
ART DIRECTOR: BARBARA NESSIM
CLIENT: COLLIER GRAPHIC SERVICES

**525**
ARTIST: **BARBARA NESSIM**
ART DIRECTOR: BARBARA NESSIM
CLIENT: COLLIER GRAPHIC SERVICES

**526**
ARTIST: **MARK PENBERTHY**

**527**
ARTIST: **ALEX MURAWSKI**    ART DIRECTOR: DAVID BARTELS    AGENCY: BARTELS & COMPANY    CLIENT: BRUCE BENDINGER

**528**
ARTIST: **DAVE LA FLEUR**

**529**
ARTIST: **GIL ASHBY**

**530**
ARTIST: **KEN JOUDREY**
ART DIRECTOR: TOLIN GREENE
CLIENT: ROCKSHOTS INC.

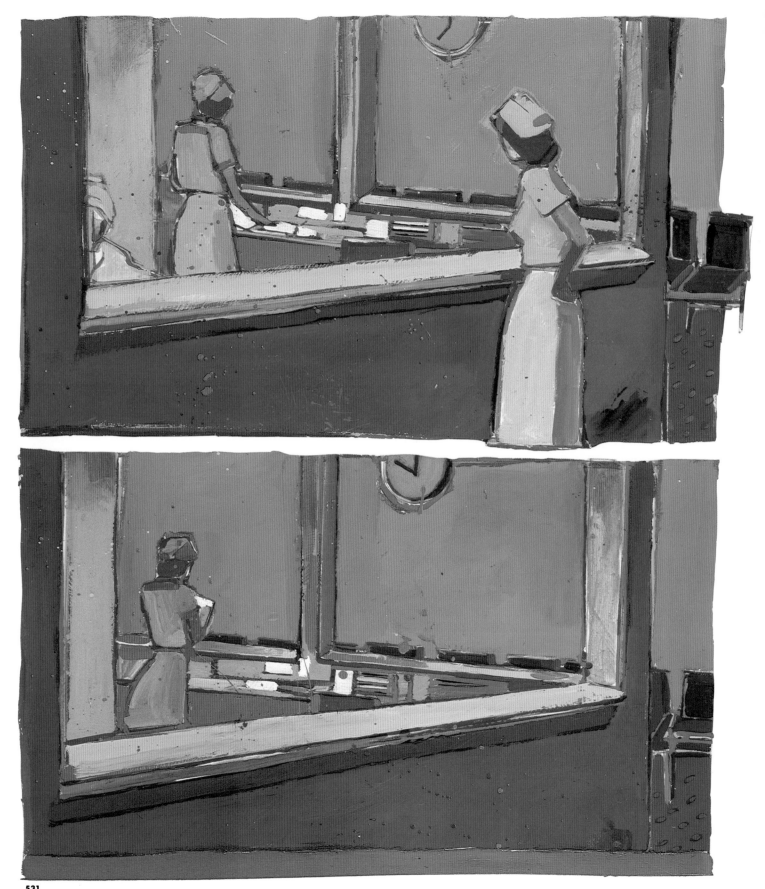

**531**
ARTIST: **JEFF SKRIMSTAD**
ART DIRECTOR: DOUG OLIVER
CLIENT: ORTHOPAEDIC HOSPITAL

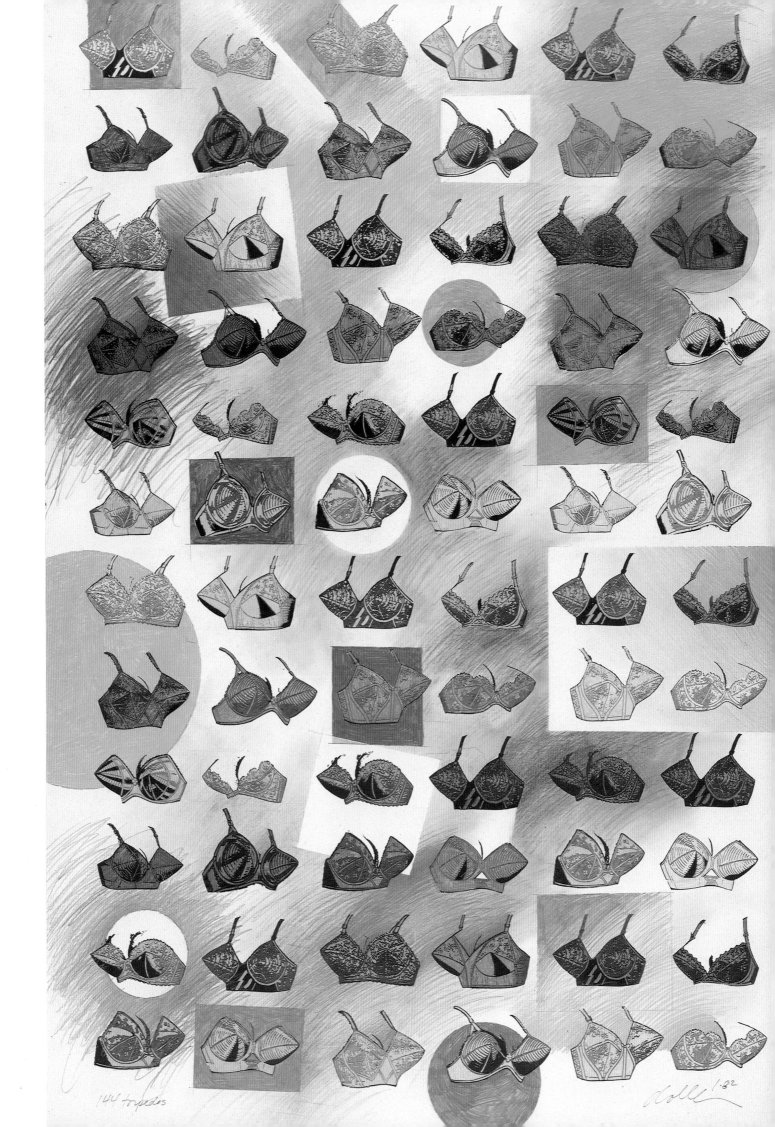

144 torpedos

**533**
ARTIST: **KAREN WATSON**
ART DIRECTOR: HEIDI PRICE
CLIENT: 9 TO 5

**536**
ARTIST: **SUSAN STILLMAN**

**537**
ARTIST: **LONNI SUE JOHNSON**
ART DIRECTOR: MICHAEL WEYMOUTH
CLIENT: WEYMOUTH DESIGN

**538**
ARTIST: **STEVE CHALKER**

**539**
ARTIST: **TIM LEWIS**
ART DIRECTOR: KIT HINRICHS
CLIENT: CHAMPION PAPER

# R I B I T

Frog went a-court-in'
and he did ride, M-hm,
Frog went a-court-in'
and he did ride, M-hm,
Frog went a-court-in'
and he did ride,
Sword and pistol
by his side, M-hm.
Rode right up to
Miss Mouse's door,
Gave three raps and
a very loud roar, M-hm.
Said he, "Miss Mouse,
are you within?"
"Yes, kind sir,
I sit and spin, M-hm."
He took Miss Mousie
on his knee,
Said, "Miss Mouse
will you marry me?"
M-hm.

"Without my Uncle
Rat's consent,
I wouldn't marry
the President, M-hm."
Uncle Rat he laughed
and shook his
fat sides,
To think his niece
would be a bride, M-hm.
Uncle Rat went a-running
down to town,
To buy his niece
a wedding gown, M-hm.
"Where shall the wedding
supper be?"
"Way down yonder in
the hollow tree," M-hm.
"What shall the wedding
supper be?"
"A fried mosquito and
a black-eyed pea,"
M-hm.

**540**
ARTIST: **MICHAEL DAVID BROWN**
ART DIRECTOR: MICHAEL DAVID BROWN

**541**
ARTIST: **LEE SIEVERS**
ART DIRECTOR: DEBE WERNER
CLIENT: ORKIN

542
ARTIST: **JOYCE KITCHELL**    ART DIRECTOR: DENNIS GILLASPY/CHERYL WOODS    CLIENT: JOYCE KITCHELL

**544**

ARTIST: **JAMES E. TENNISON**

ART DIRECTOR: JAMES E. TENNISON
CLIENT: THE SUZANNE BROWN COLLECTION

**545**

ARTIST: **GARY KELLEY**

ART DIRECTOR: GARY KELLEY
CLIENT: CEDAR RAPIDS SYMPHONY

**543**

ARTIST: **JEFF LARAMORE**

ART DIRECTOR: JEFF LARAMORE
AGENCY: YOUNG & LARAMORE
CLIENT: INDIANAPOLIS CHAMBER OF COMMERCE

**546**
ARTIST: **BURT KRAVITZ**
ART DIRECTOR: BEVERLY LITTLEWOOD/BURT KRAVITZ
CLIENT: NEWS 4, NEW YORK

**547**
ARTIST: **LEE & MARY SIEVERS**
ART DIRECTOR: LEE SIEVERS
CLIENT: LICKETY SPLIT

**548**
ARTIST: **REGAN DUNNICK**   ART DIRECTOR: CHRIS HILL   CLIENT: HILL DESIGN

**549**
ARTIST: **JOHN RUSH**    ART DIRECTOR: DAVID BARTELS    AGENCY: BARTELS & COMPANY    CLIENT: ANHEUSER-BUSCH

**550**
ARTIST: **BARBARA BANTHIEN**

ART DIRECTOR: BENNETT ROBINSON/PETER DEUTSCH
CLIENT: CONSOLIDATED FOODS CORPORATION

**551**
ARTIST: **JEFFREY J. SMITH**

ART DIRECTOR: MAXINE DAVIDOWITZ
CLIENT: REDBOOK MAGAZINE

## SCIENCE FICTION EXHIBITION

Isaac Asimov's introduction to this special juried exhibition made a point of noting the importance of the art to the text. In "Pictorial Foresight" he said: "Where the writer might be cautiously fuzzy...the illustrator had to be specific. The man who draws a futuristic scene now may be contributing to making that scene actual fact eventually." The over 110 works selected for this show were futuristic indeed, many in the realm of the fantastic. Images of spacesuited dolphins, alien housewives, 2010, metallic sea monsters and outerspace wildlife created an exhibition of rare variety and vitality. The illustrations were commissioned primarily for the editorial and book market, but some advertising, record jacket and movie poster art were also shown. The Society wishes to thank the Co-Chairmen: Wayne Barlowe and Michael Whelan; the distinguished jury: Marshall Arisman, Ken Davies, Vin DiFate, Diane Dillon, Walt Reed, John Schoenherr, Baird Searles, Murray Tinkelman, Elizabeth Woodson, Rudolph Zallinger and Dr. Louis A. Zona; and the Co-Chairmen of the two day lecture/symposium on the subject of Science Fiction: Jane Sterrett and Geoffrey Moss.

## PICTORIAL FORESIGHT
### By Isaac Asimov

In the most recent shuttle flight early in 1984, one of the astronauts ventured out into space without a tether. He was a totally independent human being moving this way and that thanks to short bursts of rocket exhaust and, eventually, found his way back to the ship. A photograph of him alone in space was a sensation.

What was sensational to me about it was how unsensational it was. I am a science fiction writer and I have been writing stories involving space travel for 45 years now. I tried to be scientific about it and I think I avoided most of the more blatant errors; however I was, at best, approximate.

What we sometimes forget, however, is that science fiction stories in the magazines are illustrated, and it was up to the science fiction illustrator to put into visual images the words composed by the science fiction writer.

Where the writer might be cautiously fuzzy ("he donned his bulky spacesuit") an illustrator—unless he could indulge in abstraction, which magazines generally do not allow—had to be specific. The spacesuit had to be shown with every knob and appurtenance in clear view. And what they showed was precisely what astronauts wear today. The illustration of the shuttle astronaut in space without a tether might have knocked the average American dead, but to me it closely resembled an illustration of the 1930's in Amazing or Astounding.

The very first story I ever had published ("Marooned Off Vesta," in the March, 1939, issue of Amazing) was illustrated by R. Fuqua. My story was rather more than a trifle amateurish. It dealt with improbabilities (a meteor strike that left a large part of the spaceship intact, including a huge water tank) and with what I suspect are impossibilities (anti-gravity).

The illustration, however, was much more credible. It showed a man in a space-suit clinging to the outer hull of a smashed spaceship and the realism, in the light of nearly half a century's hindsight, is indisputable. What's more, the astronaut in the spaceship is firing what I called a "heat-ray" at the hull, trying to puncture it—and it looks very much the way a portable laser-beam generator might look.

Illustrations may by some readers be considered an adjunct to the science fiction story which is "the main thing," but no one can avoid looking at them, and being, at least subliminally, affected by them.

Many people who work seriously on high-tech projects may, in their younger days, have been science fiction readers. (In fact, I consider that virtually certain.) They would then have seen, however glancingly, science fiction illustrations and would, however unconsciously, have retained them.

The artist, then, who pictures and makes concrete a writer's words, may be guiding the mind and hand of the technologist who, a generation later, may be engaged in designing something science fictional brought to reality. To be sure, the necessities of engineering and economics will dictate the shape and form of a robot (for instance) but so, surely, will that sense of "rightness" that may have been gained from the illustrations that had once burnt into him.

To be sure, most science fiction illustrations are (often deliberately) fantastic in conception, but there is attempted realism, too. So it comes about, and by no means in any mysterious way, that the man who draws a futuristic scene now may be contributing to making that scene actual fact eventually.

James Gurney, "Sea Monster"

John Berkey, "Space Station"

Wayne Barlowe, "Lightfall"

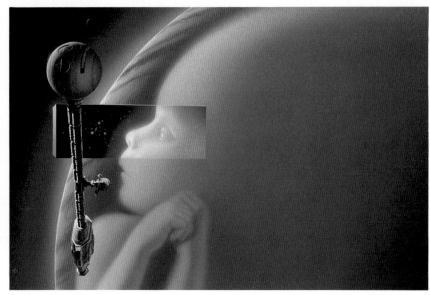

Michael Whelan, "2010: Odyssey Two"

Gregory Harris, "Lochness"

Kevin Gunnins, "Space Limbo"

Glenn Harrington, "The Flood"

Pamela Lee, "Mercury Probe"

Science Fiction Exhibition Co-Chairman, Wayne Barlowe (left) and Matt Tepper, AD, Avon Books

Science Fiction Exhibition Co-Chairman, Michael Whelan

photos: Constance Witt

Paul Alexander, "Tales of Ten Worlds"

Murray Tinkelman, "Grendel"

# SOCIETY OF ILLUSTRATORS ACTIVITIES

## ERIC EXHIBITION

The exhibition of Eric (Carl Erickson, 1891-1958), the internationally famous *Vogue* artist of the 1920s through the 1950s provided an opportunity to re-appreciate the draftmanship of this great talent.

Not only was Eric a superb fashion artist (top designers fought to have him draw their creations), but he was also a master portrait artist and accurate reporter of the contempory scene in London, Paris and New York. He was represented in all three artistic areas in this comprehensive exhibition. What *Vogue* reported, Eric depicted with sophistication, style and honesty.

Eric was elected to the Hall of Fame in 1983.

Over 90 works, assembled from many private collections, were displayed: the *Vogue* Condé Nast publishers, Bill Blass, Fashion Institute of Technology, *Gourmet* magazine, Jane Strong, and many others were major contributors.

Many members of the Society loaned drawings: Jean Cunningham, Bob Crozier, Jim Dickerson, Janet McCaffery, Al Pimsler, Irene Richards, Janet and Art Weithas.

The Society wishes to thank Barbara McKibbin, Executive Editor of *Vogue*, and Jack Potter for their assistance and support.

1936 *Vogue* Cover featuring velvet "Schiaparelli Red" hat, Courtesy Janet and Art Weithas

"The Fitting, Paris, 1948," Courtesy of Joe Eula

# SOCIETY OF ILLUSTRATORS ACTIVITIES

## OLYMPICS '84:
### The Illustrator and the LA Games

Illustrators have been hard at work for the past few years on a myriad of projects leading up to the XXIII Olympiad. Over 60 of their works were on display in this exhibition. Bob Peak's postal stamps and promotions, Bob Heindel's oil pastels for Champion Paper, Bob Ziering's "art in motion" and the six poster series for ABC-TV were among the highlights. To show the wide range of uses for art for the games, animation, medallions designed by Salvador Dali, posters and computer art were shown. Editorial art for *Sports Illustrated, Los Angeles Magazine, Life* and *National Geographic* offered a view of yet another use of illustration to promote the 1984 Summer Olympics.

Robert Heindel, "Men's 400 meter Freestyle," © 1984, Champion International Inc.

Bob Peak, "Men's Discus"

Robert M. Cunningham, "The Olympic Tradition Continues...", © 1984 ABC Inc.

# SOCIETY OF ILLUSTRATORS ACTIVITIES

## WORLD WAR I EXHIBITION
## World War I: The Illustrator Over There

"The shock and the loss and the bitterness and the blood of it," was Harvey Dunn's description of this conflict. His work and that of 25 other artists presented a picture, both heroic and horrible, of war. The Society's extensive effort with the Division of Pictorial Publicity was documented through the posters created at home for the war effort and through photos and letters from the eight AEF artists with the troops in France. Originals by Kerr Eby, N. C. Wyeth, J. C. Leyendecker, George Bellows, Dean Cornwell and Howard Chandler Christy emphasized, as Charles Dana Gibson said, "No artist is too great to come and give his best." A touching, animated videotape by James McMullan ("December 25, 1914," for PBS-TV) added a final somber note to the exhibition.

N. C. Wyeth (1882-1945), "Surrender!"

James Montgomery Flagg (1877-1960), "I Want You," U.S. Army Recruiting Poster, 1917

Harvey Dunn (1884-1952), "The AEF in Action," France, 1918

# SOCIETY OF ILLUSTRATORS ACTIVITIES

## ONE MAN/WOMAN SHOWS

**T**he three galleries of the Society provide an opportunity for members to display their artwork, either commercial or personal, to the public and to their peers. The exhibitions were in every media from wash to guache, from the humorous to the serious, by new members and past presidents. The high quality of the artwork gave mute testimony to the abilities of the exhibiting artists.

Space limits the reproduction of all but a few examples of the excellent shows presented throughout the year. Additional exhibitors were: Milton Charles, Joe Ciardiello, Bud Hawes, William Hosner, Todd Schorr, Brooke Steadman and Walter Wright.

Wendell Minor, Chairman of the Exhibition Committee, and Mitchell Hooks, Chairman of Gallery Three, did an excellent job of presenting these various exhibitions.

Birney Lettick, "Chuck Yeager Breaks The Sound Barrier," Gallery Two

Howard Munce, "The Night the Comics Bombed at the Palace," Gallery Three

Jane Sterrett, "Gandhi," Gallery Three

Robert J. Lee, "Zebra Ritual," Gallery Three

Linda Crockett, "A Ringside Seat for Life," Gallery One

Judy Clifford, "Act of Darkness," Gallery Three

Kinuko Craft, "The Gold Trumpeter," Gallery One

Wendell Minor, "The Seventh Child," Gallery One

# SOCIETY OF ILLUSTRATORS ACTIVITIES

## ANNUAL SCHOLARSHIP COMPETITION

**T**he process of creating the Society of Illustrators Annual Scholarship Competition for 1984 began in the classrooms and studios of the 110 college level institutions which entered the show. It also began with over 3700 blank canvases and sketch pads which eventually became the slides for the juries' consideration.

It is a heady task to select the 186 best works. Many strong concepts and many well rendered ideas must necessarily fall to the side. But those which melded these two aspects of art rose to the top.

The Society applauds the efforts of the students and art instructors whose talents and direction were evident in the high quality of the entries. It bodes well for the future of illustration that not only are there many naturally gifted young artists at work in America today but that there are also many fine academic institutions nurturing that talent.

We are also grateful to Hallmark Cards Inc., Lila Acheson Wallace, The Starr Foundation and others for their continued support.

D. L. CRAMER, Ph.D.
*President, Society of Illustrators*

Mickey Paraskevas receiving his Scholarship award from D. L. Cramer, President of the Society.

Alvin J. Pimsler, Scholarship Show Chairman, addressing the students and guests at the Awards Presentation.

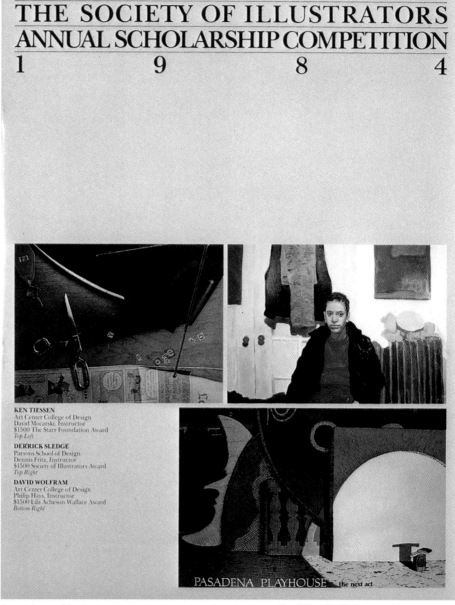

# THE SOCIETY OF ILLUSTRATORS
# ANNUAL SCHOLARSHIP COMPETITION
## 1 9 8 4

**KEN TIESSEN**
Art Center College of Design
David Mocarski, Instructor
$1500 The Starr Foundation Award
*Top Left*

**DERRICK SLEDGE**
Parsons School of Design
Dennis Fritz, Instructor
$1500 Society of Illustrators Award
*Top Right*

**DAVID WOLFRAM**
Art Center College of Design
Philip Hays, Instructor
$1500 Lila Acheson Wallace Award
*Bottom Right*

PASADENA PLAYHOUSE the next act

The catalogue of the Student Scholarship Show offered a fitting farewell to Al Pimsler "for his contributions to the arts, his dedication and service in the field of education, and especially for his efforts on behalf of the student shows." On stepping down as Chairman of the Scholarship Committee, to Al we fondly say, "Thank You."
Catalogue of Annual Scholarship Competition designed by Bernadette Evangelist.

Donors to the Society's Scholarship Fund being honored at a luncheon at the Society. (l. to r.) front: Arch Unruh, Hallmark; Deirdre DeVey, Hallmark; Alvin J. Pimsler, Show Chairman; Jeanne Bates, Hallmark; top: John Henderson, Hallmark; Bill Tinker, Hallmark; Garry Glissmeyer, Hallmark; Robert H. Blattner, Lila Acheson Wallace Fund *(Reader's Digest)*.

photos: Constance Witt

# SOCIETY OF ILLUSTRATORS ACTIVITIES

## GOVERNMENT SERVICES

**E**ach of the armed services of the United States maintains a collection of art telling the story of its part in the nation's history.

Since 1954 the Society of Illustrators has played a pivotal role in the ongoing creation of the Air Force Art Collection. Professional artists are selected from the membership and offered the opportunity to visit, witness and participate in specified Air Force missions and to record their impressions through art. The artist is free to choose his own subjects and to create the art he feels most appropriate for the collection.

Each artist travels and participates under invitational orders from the Secretary of the Air Force. In return for travel and expenses, the artist donates his time and talents and ownership of the artworks to the United States Government.

Since the 1983 Air Force Art Presentation, when Society of Illustrators members contributed 48 works of juried art, approximately 20 of our artists have visited Air Force Installations and participated in Air Force Operations. These have ranged from the final mission of the Airborne Laser Laboratory at Kirtland AFB, New Mexico, to airlift of troops into Grenada; SAC B-52/Air Launched Cruise Missile activities at Griffiss AFB, New York, F-15 operations of the 1st Tactical Fighter Wing at Langley AFB, Virginia, airlift to Lages Field, the Azores and an inspection tour visiting military airlift command facilities in England, Germany and Spain including visits to both East and West Berlin. We look forward to an exciting 1985 Air Force Art Presentation.

We have completed our first year of association with the United States Coast Guard in which five of our artists visited Coast Guard facilities in Connecticut, Massachusetts, New Jersey, Texas and California. Members participated in missions involving helicopters as well as coastal and seagoing vessels. Unlike our Air Force Program in which the artists' time and talents are donated to the government, our new Coast Guard Illustration program (COGILL) operates on an honorarium basis. Seven exciting professional works of art have been created in our initial efforts. We look forward to a continuing pleasant and successful association with the Coast Guard.

Marbury Brown, "Cuban Hardcores, Grenada, 1984," Military Airlift Command operations, U.S. Air Force Art Program.

## POSTMASTER GENERAL'S DINNER

**T**he Society has long recognized the impact and importance of U.S. Postal Stamps; and its membership has contributed in great ambers to that effort. Since the inception in 1957 of the Citizens Stamp Advisory Committee, over 60 members have created over 300 stamp designs.

William F. Bolger, Postmaster General, was honored with a dinner at the Society for his role in raising the quality of stamp design to a new level. Stevan Dohanos and Bradbury Thompson of the Citizens Committee announced at that dinner the creation of a collection within the Society of U.S. Postal issues. Mr. Bolger was also presented with a portrait by Chris Calle which was designed into a stamp.

Mr. Bolger thanked the Society and especially the artists whose talents are being more widely appreciated through stamps.

photo: Constance Witt

(l. to r.) Chris Calle, artist; Mr. Bolger; Stevan Dohanos and Bradbury Thompson of the Citizens' Stamp Advisory Committee.

# SOCIETY OF ILLUSTRATORS ACTIVITIES

## TRAVELING EXHIBITIONS TO UNIVERSITIES AND MUSEUMS

Catalogue of Traveling Exhibition, designed by Braldt Bralds, illustration by Vivienne Flesher.

**N**inety works, which were part of the 26th Annual Exhibition held in the Museum, comprised two traveling shows which allowed a wider audience to view the original work of contemporary illustrators. Forty of these works were at seven college-level galleries on the West Coast. Fifty originals traveled to Japan for exhibition in various display facilities there. Among the artists to be shown were award winners Brad Holland, Herb Tauss, Max Ginsburg and Milton Glaser. Works by Bernie Fuchs, Braldt Bralds, Carol Wald, Regan Dunnick, Matt Mahurin, Marshal Arisman and Seymour Chwast were also included.

These Traveling Exhibitions, now in their second year, have proven to be an exciting outreach program for the Society's Museum. The seven host schools were:

LIBERTY HOUSE, HONOLULU, HAWAII
ACADEMY OF ART COLLEGE,
    SAN FRANCISCO, CALIFORNIA
SAN JOSE STATE UNIVERSITY, SAN JOSE,
    CALIFORNIA
SCHOOL OF VISUAL CONCEPTS, SEATTLE,
    WASHINGTON
BOISE STATE UNIVERSITY, BOISE, IDAHO
SPOKANE FALLS COMMUNITY COLLEGE,
    SPOKANE, WASHINGTON
BRIGHAM YOUNG UNIVERSITY,
    PROVO, UTAH

In addition, loans from the Society's Permanent Collection were exhibited at the following museums: Hudson River Museum, Longview (VA) Fine Arts Center, Wesport-Weston Arts Council, U.S.C.G. Academy, Dallas Historical Society, The Portfolio and Gracie Mansion.

## OTHER EDUCATIONAL ACTIVITIES

**I**n addition to the Student Scholarship Show and catalogue, the Society was again involved in the nurturing of young talent. It continued its support of the Police Athletic League art competition through matching grants to a growing endowment. A. I. Friedman Company's art supply contribution supplemented that grant.

The Scholastic Art Awards Competition selected Brent Mueller of Tremper High School, Kenosha, WI, to receive their "Young American Artist for 1984" award. He was honored with a luncheon at the Society.

An enthusiastic class from the New School for Social Research toured the Society and heard lectures and slide presentations on the history of illustration. These students were enrolled in the course titled: "New York's Unusual Museums."

Society Director, Terrence Brown, lecturing a class from The New School, on the History of American Illustration. The course: New York's Unusual Museums.

## SYMPOSIUM

**A** two-evening symposium on the art of Science Fiction, "A Trip to the Moon," was an exciting dialogue on the roots and future of that genre. Wayne Barlowe, Vin DiFate and Baird Searles served as one panel; Don Munson, Walt Reed and Sandra Fillipucci served as the second panel. Ms. Fillipucci was escorted by a 6'2" robot that brought Science Fiction into Science Fact. Jane Sterrett and Geoffrey Moss moderated the two evenings.

## EVENING SKETCH CLASSES

**T**he evening sketch sessions on life, fashion and portrait drawing were well attended by both members and the public. Professional models provided an opportunity for artists to practice their skills.

## JOINT ETHICS COMMITTEE

**S**ince 1945, the Joint Ethics Committee has served the Graphic Industry by providing an alternative to litigation in the settlement of ethic disputes through peer review, mediation and arbitration.

Our six sponsors are the most respected professional organizations in the field: Society of Illustrators, The Art Directors Club, American Society of Magazine Photographers, Society of Photographers and Artists Representatives, Graphic Artists Guild, and the American Institute of Graphic Arts.

Selected representatives from these organizations serve as volunteers on the Committee. The services of the JEC are offered free of charge, and are available to anyone in the communications industry.

The JEC has formulated a Code of Fair Practice which outlines the accepted ethical standards for the Graphics Industry. Send $2.50 for Code booklet or for further information please write to: Joint Ethics Committee, P.O. Box 179, Grand Central Station, New York, N.Y. 10163.

# INDEX

## ARTISTS

## ART DIRECTORS

# INDEX

## MAGAZINES, PUBLISHERS & PUBLICATIONS

## AGENCIES

**BILL ERLACHER** ARTISTS ASSOCIATES

ARTISTS REPRESENTED

NORMAN ADAMS

DON BRAUTIGAM

MICHAEL DEAS

MARK ENGLISH

ALEX GNIDZIEJKO

ROBERT HEINDEL

STEVE KARCHIN

DICK KREPEL

SKIP LIEPKE

RICK McCOLLUM

FRED OTNES

DANIEL SCHWARTZ

211 EAST 51 STREET, NEW YORK, NEW YORK 10022 (212) 755-1365/6 ASSOCIATE: NICOLE EDELL

# S T E V E ◆ K A R C H I N

c.1985

BOXES ◆ COLLAGES

REPRESENTED BY ◆ BILL ERLACHER, ARTISTS ASSOCIATES ◆ 211 EAST 51 STREET ◆ N.Y., N.Y. 10022 ◆ (212) 755-1365/6

**MARK ENGLISH**
has received the most awards ever
given to an artist by the Society of Illustrators
in their Annual Exhibitions. He was elected to
the Society's Hall of Fame in 1983.

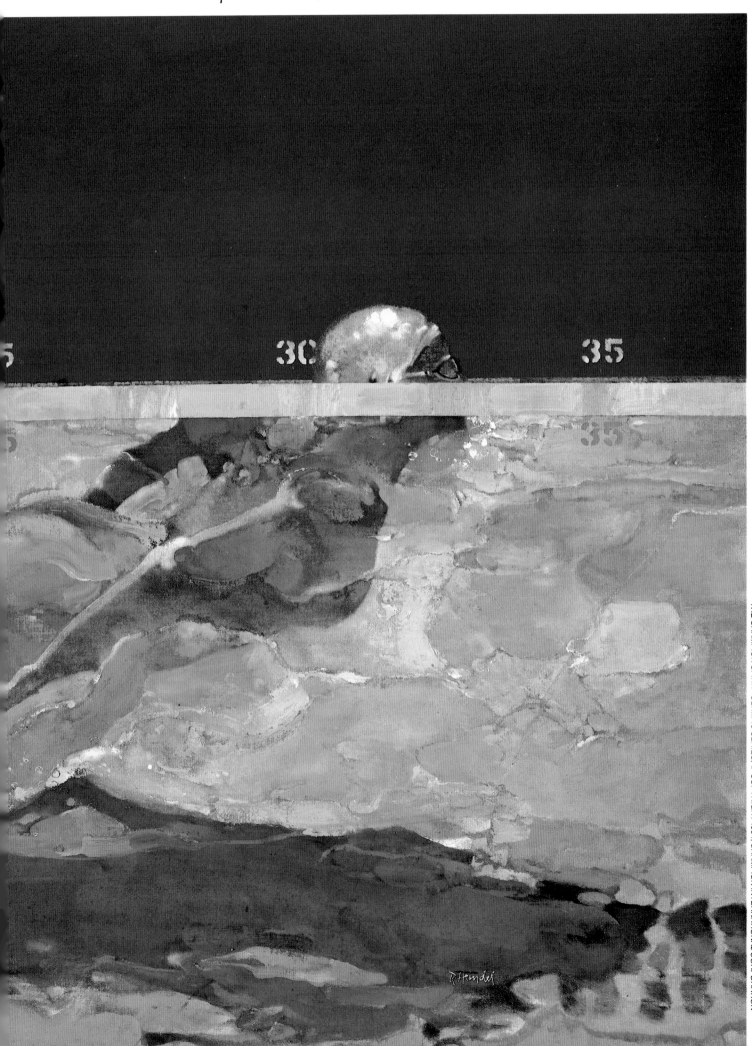

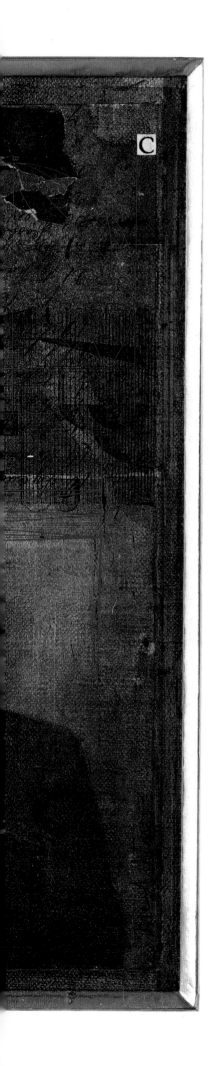

## FRED OTNES

"His is a fine art of construction, whether he is building images on a square of canvas or in the architecture of a three-dimensional construction. It is a very specific mastery of space, and of the relationships of elements within it, exercised in a very concrete way. Using both raw clippings and film negatives projected onto the working surface, he experiments in form and scale, thus constructing each piece image by image. This personal control is essential in achieving the blend of old and new so persistent in his work, an aura of timelessness which may well be the key to its enduring popularity."

—Rose DeNeve
Print Magazine

OIL                              "THE PRESSERS"                              22" X 26"

# SKIP LIEPKE

REPRESENTED BY BILL ERLACHER

OIL            "THE DRESSMAKERS SHOP"            30" X 40"

# D I C K
# KREPEL

© 1984, ARTISTS ASSOCIATES

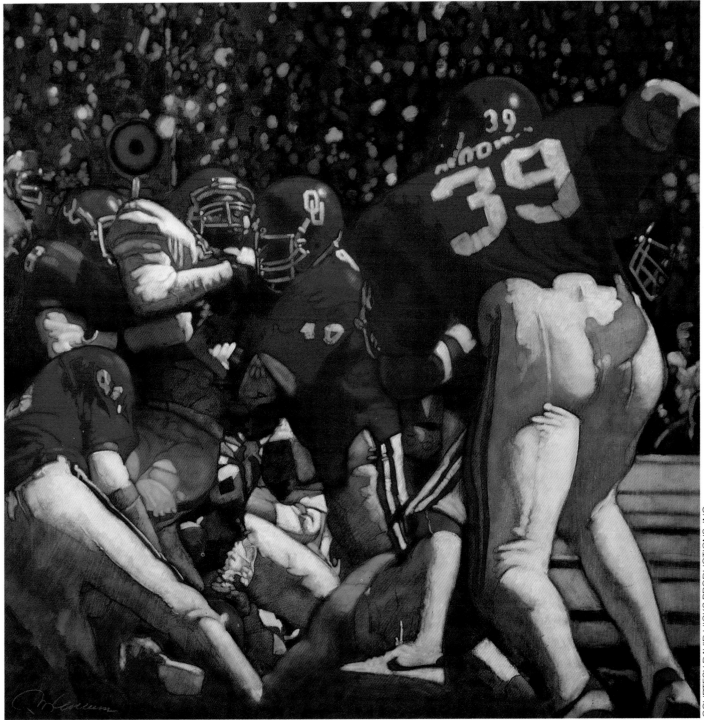

"Defense", by Rick McCollum, serves as a colorful reminder that spring drills dominate Owen Field during the month of April as a harbinger of fall, when a new season and another challenging schedule will arrive to excite Oklahoma players, coaches and fans. McCollum's illustrations have appeared in leading magazines both in the United States and abroad. Publishers such as Random House, Time-Life, Macmillan, Bantam and more have utilized his talents, as have the major American television networks and numerous business corporations. Georgia Pacific commissioned the artist to produce a set of 12 sports paintings for a calendar and his work also has appeared on ad campaigns for resorts and ski schools at Aspen, Colorado.

BILL ERLACHER, ARTISTS ASSOCIATES, 211 EAST 51 STREET, NEW YORK, NEW YORK 10022. TELEPHONE: (212) 755-1365/6

# RAPIDOGRAPH®

## *. . . Feathers and Flora by Kathy Spalding*

Kathy Spalding, a commercial illustrator and fine-artist, relies on Rapidograph® pens for maximum drawing time when creating her large drawings for many subject categories, including this "gallery" of exotic birds. The quality of detailing she achieves with her Rapidograph® pens provides a nearly three-dimensional perception of these birds, whether in their lush, tropical habitat or silhouetted, as in the case of the ritualistic cranes. The cranes, by the way, are from a series of lavish drawings with oriental inscriptions, suggesting the brush-and-ink technique of Japanese *sumi-e*.

Most of artist Spalding's drawings are finished and reproduced as black ink-line art, with a few selected subjects enhanced with watercolor washes. On some origi-nals, she adds color before litho-graphing an edition of prints. Her Rapidograph® pens accompany her far and wide, including Antarctica and The Amazon, to draw wildlife subjects.

Dependability and ease of per-formance are the reasons Rapido-graph® pens are the most widely used technical pens in the United States and Canada. The patented DRY DOUBLE-SEAL® cap keeps ink throughout the balanced ink-flow system ready for instant startup.

Tubular nib (available in 13 line widths) allows the Rapidograph® pen to move in any direction on virtually any drawing surface, in-cluding acetate and glass, with the ease of a pencil, making it far more versatile and comfortable to use than crow quill or other pen types.

For the satisfaction of time well spent with your own pen-and-ink draw-ing technique, be sure you see *Koh-I-Noor Rapidograph®* on the pen. Accept no substitutes.

"Get-acquainted" packaging (Product No. 3165-BX) offers a special saving with pen/ink combi-nation. Single pens and pen sets are also available. Ask your dealer or send the coupon for details: Koh-I-Noor Rapidograph, Inc., Bloomsbury, NJ 08804  (201) 479-4124.  In Canada: 1815 Meyerside Dr., Mississauga, Ont. L5T 1G3 (416) 671-0696.

# ART

These drawings by Kathy Spalding are copyrighted by the artist and may not be reproduced for any reason without written permission from the artist.

## KOH-I-NOOR
### RAPIDOGRAPH®

Please send complimentary Catalog "E" describing Rapidograph technical pens, Koh-I-Noor and Pelikan inks and other artist materials.

☐ Please send me the names of Koh-I-Noor dealers in my area.

Name _____
(please print or type)

Company _____

Address _____

City _____ State _____ Zip_____

**KOH-I-NOOR RAPIDOGRAPH, INC.**
100 North St., Bloomsbury, NJ 08804

In Canada: 1815 Meyerside Drive
Mississauga, Ont. L5T 1G3

# It Takes Masters To Make Masters...

MARSHALL ARISMAN  
*LARRY BAKKE  
JOE BOWLER  
MILTON CHARLES  
BERNIE D'ANDREA  
PAUL DAVIS  
ROBERT GROSSMAN  
RICHARD HARVEY  
DOUG JOHNSON  
MARVIN MATTLESON  
FRANKLIN McMAHON  
WILSON McCLEAN  
JAMES McMULLEN

JACQUI MORGAN  
DON IVAN PUNCHATZ  
DAVE PASSALAQUA  
REYNOLD RUFFINS  
LEE SAVAGE  
ISADORE SELTZER  
TOM SGOUROS  
BARON STOREY  
MURRAY TINKLEMAN*  
JOHN VARGO*  
ROBERT WEAVER  
CHUCK WILKENSON  
Resident Faculty*

Some of the greatest names in Illustration, what else do they have in common? They have all been summer faculty in Syracuse University's Independent Study Master of Fine Arts in Illustration program.

The Syracuse program is designed for the professional who wants to continue working full time yet improve his skills and earn a degree in a relatively short period. The program is intensive, you'll be challenged, moved out of your rut, and you'll grow, grow, grow. If you'd like to spend a few weeks a year working with some of the top professionals while earning an MFA degree:

call or write  
Syracuse University,  
(315) 423 3269

Independent Study Degree Programs  
Rm 302 Reid Hall, 610 East Fayette St.,  
Syracuse, N. Y., 13210

Morgan Kane

Guy Hoff

Howard Chandler Christy

Harrison Fisher

Bradshaw Crandell

Joseph Du Port

barnett plotkin · 230 east 44 st · n.y., n.y. 10017 · (212) 661 · 7149

## Chuck Hamrick

Peter Fiore

*Jeffrey Terreson*

## Rob Sauber

## Attila Hejja

## Jonathan Milne

## Thierry Thompson

## Jeffrey Mangiat

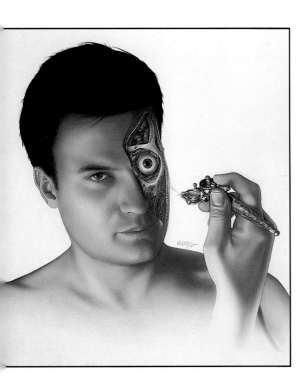

## Dan Brown

## Joel Spector

## Carl Cassler

## Mitchell Hooks

## Jim Campbell

## John Eggert

## Bob Berran

David Schleinkofer

Mark Watts

Geoff McCormack

Mike Noome

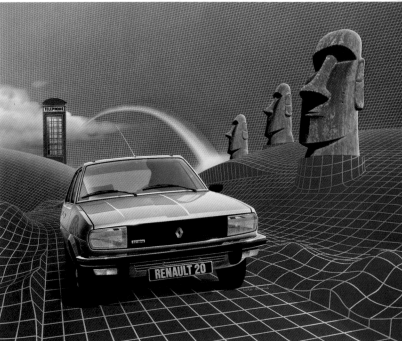

## Mike Mikos

## Dave Kilmer

## Jim Deneen

## Jack Jones

## Chris Notarile

## Dennis Lyall

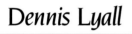

## Paul Tankersley

## Bob Jones

## Wally Neibart

## Michael Smollin

## Cliff Spohn

## Ben Wohlberg

# 64
## REASONS TO ATTEND

## THE ILLUSTRATORS & DESIGNERS WORKSHOP

The faculty:
Alan E. Cober,
Mark English,
Bernie Fuchs,
Bob Heindel,
Fred Otnes,
Robert Peak,
Seymour Chwast,
John deCesare,
Alan Peckolick.
Past guests include:
Lorraine Allen,
Sam Antupit,
Darwin Bahm,
Walter Bernard,
Roger Black,
Herb Bleiweiss,
Ahden Busch,
Jacquelin Casey,
Dick Coyne,
Kinuko Y. Craft,
Jacqueline Dedell,
Etienne Delessert,
Harry O. Diamond,
Leo and Diane Dillon,
Bill Erlacher,
Gordon Fisher,
Phyllis Flood,
Dick Gangel,
Fritz Gottschalk,
Rudy Hoglund,
Nigel Holmes,
Judeth Jampel,

The Workshop includes presentations by the
faculty and guests, visits to the studios
and offices of faculty members, one-to-one
portfolio reviews, demonstrations and crits
of a live assignment, issued to registrants
prior to the event.

Write for more detailed information to:
The Illustrators Workshop Inc.
P.O. Box 3447, Noroton, CT 06820 U.S.A.
(203) 655-8394

Harvey Kahn,
Herb Lubalin,
Robert L. Mayotte,
Rick McCollum,
Gerald McConnell,
Wilson McLean,
David Merrill,
Susan E. Meyer,
Duane Michals,
Eugene Mihaesco,
Lou Myers,
Barbara Nessim,
Jack O'Grady,
Howard Paine,
George Parker,
Al Parker,
Art Paul,
Martin Pedersen,
Margery Peters,
Jerry Pinkney,
Don Ivan Punchatz,
Walt Reed,
Jeffrey Schrier,
Leslie Segal,
Maurice Sendak,
Neil Shakery,
Lou Silverstein,
Elwood H. Smith,
Donald Smolen,
Ed Soyka,
Atha Tehon,
Jessica Weber,
Mary Zisk.

# Kirchoff/Wohlberg, Inc.
## Artists Representative

866 United Nations Plaza
New York, NY 10017
212-644-2020

897 Boston Post Road
Madison, CT 06443
203-245-7308

# OUR TEN COMMANDMENTS of ARTIST REPRESENTATION

1. We represent only artists we believe in and are totally committed to them.

2. We believe in being more than agents and become involved in the *total career* of the artists we represent.

3. We appreciate the problems of the artist and try, whenever possible, to alleviate these problems.

4. We also appreciate the problems of the art director: his client-agency relationship, tight deadlines and budget limitations and try to help him solve these problems whenever we can.

5. We believe in *full representation.* That means taking on only that number of artists that we can fully represent as well as insuring that each artist is non-competitive in style with other artists we represent.

6. We believe in giving *full service* to our artists and to the art director, promptly and professionally. Every client, no matter what the job price, deserves the very best we can offer.

7. We believe in being *flexible.* Business conditions change. The economy rises and falls. Accounts switch. We and our artists must adjust to all changes in order to successfully survive.

8. We believe in always meeting deadlines and always keeping a bargain. We and our artists are only as good as our word and our last job.

9. We believe in *BEING HONEST* at all times. With our artists. With the art director. With ourselves.

10. And finally, we believe in our *profession...* the profession of representing artists. We firmly believe that it is the most exciting and challenging profession anywhere and we are proud to be a part of it.

Barbara Gordon
Associates Ltd.
165 East 32 Street
New York, N.Y. 10016
212-686-3514

PANORAMA 1

*William Hosner
Illustrations*

450 West Fort Street
Detroit, Michigan 48226
313•962•0405

New York Tel.:
Carol Chislovsky
212•980•3510

*Alan E. Cohen*

*B. Fuchs*

*Gerstein*

# NICHOLAS GAETANO
## WILSON McLEAN:

*B. Peak*

*Isadore Seltzer*

*N. Walker*

**Harvey Kahn
Associates, Inc.**

*50 East 50th St. New York, NY 10022
212 752-8490*

*Doug Kahn, Associate*

**A**

**B**

**C**

# MADISON SQUARE PRESS

## A selection of significant books being offered at great discounts!

Essential reference sources for photographers, artists, graphic designers and buyers. Some of these volumes offer important business and legal guides—others present outstanding examples of art, photography and graphic design by the nation's leading talents. A must for all in the profession. Please add $2.00 handling and postage charge for first book and $1.00 for each book thereafter. New York State residents add 8.25% sales tax.

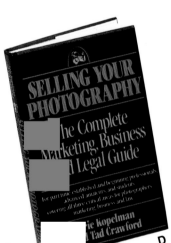

**D**

**E**

**F**

**G**

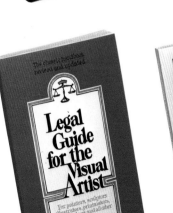

**H**

**I**

**J**

U.S. sales only:
Please add $2.50 handling and postage charge for first book and $1.00 for each book thereafter. New York State residents add 8.25% sales tax.

### A. THE ADVERTISING WORLD OF NORMAN ROCKWELL
By Donald Stoltz and Marshall Stoltz

Not only does this handsome book present a wealth of Rockwell's illustrations, but it reveals the extent of his role in advertising. The fascinating history of each advertiser is related: how the company began, its progress through the decades and the circumstances under which Rockwell was given the assignment. A bonanza for Rockwell fans and those interested in the "rags to riches" growth of major corporations. 209 pages. 8 x 10. ISBN 0-942604-04-0
List $39.95  **MSP PRICE $33.95**

### B. SOUNDS FROM THE BULLPEN
By Howard Munce

A collection of hilarious, satirical essays and drawings about the working life of commercial artists. Originally written to amuse members of the Society of Illustrators, it will also entertain art-oriented professionals and students —and all those with a sense of humor. 80 pages. 9 x 12. ISBN 0-942604-01-6
List (soft cover) $9.95   **MSP PRICE $6.95**
List (hard cover) $17.95   **MSP PRICE $9.95**
Deluxe limited edition, numbered and signed by author, in protective slipcase $25.00
**MSP PRICE $14.95**

### C. ASSEMBLAGE
By Gerald McConnell

Everything you need to know to make your own three-dimensional art—how to develop ideas, collect materials, make models, join pieces together and photograph your work for reproduction. Twenty-two commercial assignments made by the author reproduced in color. 96 pages. 8½ x 11. ISBN 0-442-25264-1
List $10.95   **MSP PRICE $7.95**

### D. SELLING YOUR PHOTOGRAPHY
By Arie Kopelman and Tad Crawford

The first and only book that equips you to earn a substantial income from photography. Clear no-nonsense guide to the three critical areas of the profession: marketing, business and law. For beginners and advanced amateurs as well as established photographers. 256 pages. 9½ x 6¼. ISBN 0-312-71255-3
List $14.95   **MSP PRICE $11.95**

### E. CORPORATE AND COMMUNICATIONS DESIGN ANNUAL
Graphic Artists Guild

A wide array of approaches taken by design firms. Essential reference for design professionals and marketing or communications managers seeking new ideas and talent. Teachers and advanced students will also find this book helpful. 80 pages. 7½ x 9½. ISBN 0-912417-02-1A
List $24.95   **MSP PRICE $12.95**

### F. ASMP BOOK 3
Professional Photography Annual

A full-color directory of the nation's most exciting professional photography. Every specialty—from aerial to underwater—is widely represented. An essential tool for every working or aspiring photographer. 472 pages. 7½ x 9½. ISBN 0-912417-03-X
List $39.95   **MSP PRICE $19.95**

### G. LEGAL GUIDE FOR THE VISUAL ARTIST, Revised Edition
by Tad Crawford

An indispensable text on the visual artists's legal problems. Covers copyright, contracts, censorship, moral rights, sales of art and reproduction rights, publishing contracts, taxation, hobby losses, estate planning and taxation, collecting and grants. Model contracts included. 256 pages. 7 x 12. ISBN 0-942604-08-3
List $16.95   **MSP PRICE $13.95**

### H. PRICING AND ETHICAL GUIDELINES (5th Edition)
Graphic Artists Guild

A must for artists and buyers who know how important it is to keep up with changes in pricing and business practices. Includes current laws affecting contract provisions, bidding on assignments, billing, collecting and record-keeping, salaries and wages, new technologies and much more. 200 pages. 7 x 12. ISBN 0-932102-05-0
List $16.95   **MSP PRICE $13.95**

### I. THE NEW ILLUSTRATION
From the Exhibition held at the Society of Illustrators

A look at the tradition-breaking show that stirred up controversy and applause. The energy explodes from these artists of the post-Viet Nam, post-industrial generation as they run the gamut from high-tech elegance to simple looniness. See the work of Mick Haggerty, Lou Beach and 88 others in full-color. 160 pages. 9½ x 9½. ISBN 0-942604-06-7
List $24.95   **MSP PRICE $21.95**

### J. DIRECTORY 4
Graphic Artists Guild

An extensive collection of illustration compiled from the Graphic Artists Guild membership. Includes a broad range of techniques and styles. Professionals as well as teachers and students will find this an invaluable reference source. 222 pages. 7½ x 9½. ISBN 0-912417-01-3A
List $25.95   **MSP PRICE $12.95**

**List title(s) and send check or money order to:**
**MADISON SQUARE PRESS, INC.**
**10 East 23rd Street, New York, NY 10010**

SOCIETY OF ILLUSTRATORS

Masterpieces of graphic art from posters, books, magazines, newspapers, and advertising art

200 YEARS OF AMERICAN ILLUSTRATION

B

THE ILLUSTRATOR IN AMERICA 1880·1980 A CENTURY OF ILLUSTRATION

Walt and Roger Reed

THE SOCIETY OF ILLUSTRATORS

A

For the first time, are being offered

TWENTY YEARS OF award winners

SOCIETY OF ILLUSTRATORS

C

# those cherished volumes at dramatic savings!

Don't miss out on this opportunity to complete your library—or to start one. Invaluable reference books for illustrators, art directors, art buyers, collectors, educators and students. An inspiration for the established professional as well as for those hoping to enter the field.

- Competitive costs
  - Flexibility in production time
    - Knowledge of sales reps
      - Service and fine quality
        - Financial stability

*Can you expect all of these from your printer ?*

*The Society of Illustrators has come to us since its annual book, "Illustrators 23."*

 DAI NIPPON is ready to serve you. You can get on the spot consultation from professional salesman.

**NEW YORK** DNP (AMERICA), INC.
Headquarters
1633 Broadway, 15th Fl.
New York, N.Y. 10019
(212) 397-1880
Graphic Printing Division

**SAN FRANCISCO** DNP (AMERICA), INC.
San Francisco Office
The Hearst Building
5 Third Street, Suite 430
San Francisco, CA 94103
(415) 788-1618

**CHICAGO** DNP (AMERICA), INC.
800 Enterprise Drive,
Suite 124, Oak Brook,
IL 60521
(312) 655-0150

**TOKYO** DAI NIPPON PRINTING COMPANY, LTD.
1-1-1 Ichigaya Kagacho, Shinjuku-ku
Tokyo, Japan 162
International Sales Division
(03) 266-3307